DEVELOPMENT – LESSONS FOR THE FUTURE

DEVELOPMENT –
LESSONS FOR THE FUTURE

By

THOMAS PATRICK MELADY

and

R. B. SUHARTONO

ORBIS BOOKS
MARYKNOLL, NEW YORK 10545

To Margaret and Vipada

1796093

Contents

Preface

Theories and programs concerned with economic development played a major role in the media when international affairs were discussed in the 1950s and the 1960s. The simple fact that emerged was that there are a few people in the world who possess most of the world's wealth.

This gap is not new, but the awareness by the poor of the world of their poverty is a most recent phenomenon. Most of the theories, however, on how to transform the impotent poor economies into productive ones have come from the developed societies. In the 1950s and the 1960s the industrialized nations, international agencies, and the developing societies were all involved in programs of economic development.

Now as we progress through the 1970s and approach the eve of the last quarter of the twentieth century, the authors of this book have withdrawn a little from the discussion of on-going schemes and programs to concentrate on the overriding fundamental issues that have emerged after two decades.

They start with a fundamental question: How do you determine which countries are developing? What do they have in common and how do they differ?

Since economic growth is the goal of most development plans, what are the factors affecting economic growth? What is the role of agriculture and what have been the results of some of the better known schemes, especially the Green Revolution?

It is important to have some commonly accepted definition of development. How do we measure the level of economic development? The authors have analyzed some of the leading examples of economic development programs of the past two decades.

Finally, since the overriding reason for this interest in economic development is man, consideration is given to man and his role in society. Here we focus on man as a producer, the role of education, the importance of nationalism, and the need for good leadership.

The views herein expressed are, of course, those of the authors, and do not necessarily represent those of the United Nations or the United States Department of State.

DEVELOPMENT – LESSONS FOR THE FUTURE

CHAPTER I

THE DEVELOPING COUNTRIES
A Nonhomogeneous Group

Introduction

In this chapter the world economy will be classified into
three broad categories in accordance with United Nations
practices: the *developing economies*; the *developed market
economies*; and the *centrally planned economies*. The
developing economies are to be regarded as market economies as well; the words "economy" and "country," on the
other hand, will be used interchangeably.

The *developed market economies* consist of Australia,
Canada, Japan, New Zealand, South Africa, the United
States, and all of western and southern Europe (including
Turkey and Yugoslavia). These are the most active trading
countries (accounting for more than two-thirds of the
world's trade), intensely penetrating each other's domestic
markets (about three-fourths of their total trade is among
themselves), producing a host of complementary and competing products, and participating in an interdependent
currencies system. The *centrally planned economies*, on
the other hand, consist of Mongolia, North Korea, North
Vietnam, the People's Republic of China, the USSR, and
the seven East European countries (including Albania).
The rest of the world, consisting of more than 100 countries, are the developing economies.

It can be noted at the outset that the group of the developing economies cannot be considered as homogeneous. Some have been politically independent for more than a century, others have not had the political tradition of unitary states prior to their dates of independence from the colonial powers. Population in a few developing economies is less than 1 million.[1] Per capita gross domestic product (GDP) figures range from around $50 or less in Burundi, Malawi, Rwanda, Somalia, and Upper Volta, to almost $5,000 in Kuwait, and greater than $1,000 in Israel and Libya.

The contribution of the manufacturing sector in GDP can be lower than 10 percent, while in a few other developing countries the figures can be greater than 20 percent.[2] The percentage of adults who are literate to total population in some is less than 8 percent, while in others it is greater than 80 percent.[3] Resource endowments among these countries also differ considerably.[4] The list can further be expanded whereby even from the narrow aspect of the quantifiable concept, it will be found that the more variables are to be introduced, the greater diversity in the values of the parameters.

In various international meetings, views have been expressed regarding the nonhomogeneous nature of the developing countries. Thus the *Charter of Algiers*[5], for example, refers to the varying stages of economic development existing among the developing countries as well as to the varying factors responsible for their development; policy measures which are required to accelerate their economic development, therefore, would differ from one developing country to another.

The Working Group of Fifteen[6], on the other hand, has noted that there are differences in income levels as well as in economic and social structure, although it is of the opinion that all developing countries are united by common denominators: the insufficiency of their rate of growth as compared to needs, and the external vulnerability of their economies. The Second Session of UNCTAD in New Delhi has recognized the differing characteristics and stages of development of the developing countries, and that the least developed among these confront special problems.[7]

The international discussions on the nonhomogeneity aspect had culminated in the drawing up of the list of the least developed among the developing countries which was subsequently adopted by the United Nations General Assembly.[8] Thus, the international community has acted on the recognition that there exists different levels of economic development even within the group of the developing countries themselves, and that the least developed among these countries need special measures in their favor.

In this chapter some selected statistical data will be presented, highlighting the differences that exist among the developing countries. The data refer to national income, the per capita value of which is commonly utilized as a measure of the level of development (although it does present some problems, to be discussed in another chapter); exports, which, together with imports and domestic savings, determine the level of domestic investment, the latter commonly regarded as the most important determinant of the rate of growth of income; and the structural aspect, viewed from the standpoint of the industrial origin of GDP. Subsequently the discussion will be focused on the predominantly agricultural developing countries. Occasionally figures for the least developed countries will be singled out in passing.

Global, Regional, and Individual Country Income Disparity

In 1969, the tentative estimate of the total gross national product (GNP) of all the market economies combined was about $2,270 billion while the total population was about 2,400 million, yielding a per capita figure of about $950. If the centrally planned economies are to be included as well, but excluding the centrally planned countries in Asia for lack of comparable data, the total GNP would be around $2,690 billion and the total population 2,750 million, giving a per capita figure of about $980.[9]

Whether income is to be measured by GDP at factor

cost or at market prices, or by GNP instead, it appears that
though they account for about two-thirds of the population
in the combined market economies, the developing countries
only produce less than one-sixth of the total income[10]:

**WORLD MARKET ECONOMIES: PERCENTAGE
DISTRIBUTION OF INCOME AND POPULATION**

Category	GDP				GNP	Population	
	factor cost			market prices			
	1950	1960	1967	1967	1969	1950	1969
All market economies	100.0	100.0	100.0	100.0	100.0	100.0	100.0
Developed	84.9	84.4	84.7	85.3	85.6	35.5	31.1
Developing	15.1	15.6	15.3	14.7	14.4	64.5	68.9

Sources: World Economic Survey 1963, 1969-1970; Review of International
Trade and Development 1970.

Accordingly, there is a great disparity in the global distribution of income, as the following table indicates:

ESTIMATES OF PER CAPITA GNP, 1969

Category	Per capita GNP in dollars
Market economies:	
Developed	2487
Developing	192
Africa	146
Other Asia[a]	125
West Asia	475
Western Hemisphere	467
Centrally planned economies[b]	1201

Source: Review of International Trade and Development, 1970.
[a]Including Iran.
[b]Excluding centrally planned economies in Asia.

The income disparity has increased over time: in 1950, per capita GDP in the developing economies was about one-tenth of the figure observed in the developed countries; in 1969, on the other hand, it was less than one-twelfth.

The table also indicates that there exists regional income disparities among the developing countries. In fact, in 1969, more than half of the population are from those countries which generate less than a quarter of the combined GNP of the whole developing economies (on the other hand, about one-fourteenth of the population are from the countries which generate around one-fourth of the total GNP). Thus, the group of developing countries with the population majority has less than $100 per capita GNP:

DEVELOPING ECONOMIES: DISTRIBUTION OF POPULATION AND NUMBER OF COUNTRIES BY LEVELS OF PER CAPITA GNP, 1969

Per capita GNP (in dollars)	Number of countries	Population (in million)
Under 51	2	8.9
51-100	23	860.5
101-150	17	187.2
151-200	8	115.6
201-300	21	178.3
301-500	14	171.8
501-1000	12	108.6
Over 1000	4	5.6

Sources: United Nations Monthly Bulletin of Statistics, April, 1972; Review of International Trade and Development, 1970; World Bank Atlas, 6th ed.

The average per capita GNP of the least developed is less than half the whole developing countries average (ranging from about $50 in Burundi, Rwanda, and Upper Volta to around $120 in Sudan, Western Samoa, and Yemen).

A very broad generalization may be noted (excluding Asian centrally planned economies). Geographically, the economically developed, politically, and socially coherent states, and relatively well-off and affluent societies are in general to be found in the Northern zone, in centrally planned and developed market economies alike, consisting of some 35 countries. On the other hand, the developing countries, consisting of more than 100 political units, exhibit different shades of political and social coherence as well as various degrees of relative poverty and affluence, and are to be found in the Southern periphery. The world economy seems to be somewhat dichotomized into the metropolitan urban center in the North and the peripheral rural ghetto in the South.

Economic power is political power. There is a growing reality that international policies are being formulated in terms of zonal geographical distinction. The stability of the mutual relations between the powers in the North is more and more considered as the determining factor for international peace and stability. There seems to be an increasing confidence that the North could contain and insulate problems and disturbances generating from the peripheral rural ghetto in the South.

Some developing countries have managed to experience rapid economic advance as measured by their increase in per capita income. However, based on 1955-65 data, it has been observed that among the developing countries, there seems to have occurred a polarization in their growth pattern, favoring the richer of these countries.[10] Although a higher than average per capita income is no assurance for greater than average rate of growth, a greater than average rate of growth of income has occurred mostly in those countries with higher than average per capita income. As has been noted earlier, the poorer economies are populated by the majority of the people in the developing countries.

Within each developing country, there is also a sharp inequality in the distribution of income, probably more so than in the developed economies (in 1957, the upper 5 percent in Mexico and Venezuela obtained 37 and 30 percent of personal income, respectively, comparable to those accrued to the upper 10 percent in the developed countries). The table on page 8 indicates that among the selected sample of countries, the upper income brackets in the developing economies have generally received a higher percentage of income than in the developed countries; it also indicates that through time, the lower income brackets share decreases in Argentina, Mexico, and Puerto Rico, while the share of the higher income brackets increases (in contrast to the reverse pattern observed in the United States).[11]

A recent study of income distribution in 44 countries has found that the average figures for percentage of income accrued to the lower 60, and upper 20 and 5 percent of population are, respectively, 26 (range: 2-35), 56 (range: 39-89), and 30 percent (range: 11-48). From the table on page 8 and these figures it might be assumed that if income distribution is taken into consideration as well, people who are poor will exceed those who can be inferred from the data of aggregate per capita income alone.

It might be conjectured that the top income groups are from sectors of economic activities that are linked more to the developed countries than to the national economies (as exemplified by the dualistic pattern in the production structures of the developing countries, where the modern and monetized sector is more oriented to the world market for generating income through exports as well as for imports of the needed commodities). It might also be suspected that in many developing countries the bulk of income of the upper strata is generated by enterprises which are owned and controlled by nonnationals.

The pattern of world order characterized by great inequality in the distribution of income is not necessarily unstable. The achievement of the mutual stability of the power relations in the North can be transmitted to the South through the latter's economic links to the former. If it so wishes, the North might be able to exert indirect ruling on the South, containing and insulating the threat of turbulence caused by mass poverty in the peripheral Southern rural ghetto.

SELECTED COUNTRIES: PERCENTAGE DISTRIBUTION
OF INCOME SHARES RECEIVED BY FAMILIES

Country	Year	Personal income of the lower income brackets, 60 percent of families	Personal income of the upper income brackets, 10 percent of families
Developing:			
Argentina	1953	32	37
	1961	31	39
Ceylon	1950	30	50[a]
Chile	1960	24	37
Ecuador	1957	36	30
India	1950	28	55[a]
Mexico	1950	25	49
	1963	21	42
Puerto Rico	1953	30	33
	1963	28	34
Venezuela	1957	16	45
Developed:			
Denmark	1952	29	31
Germany, Fed. Rep.	1950	29	34
Italy	1948	31	34
Netherlands	1950	29	35
United Kingdom	1952	34	30
United States	1952	32	31
	1962	34	28
Sweden	1948	29	30

Sources: The Economic Development of Latin America in the Post-war Period (United Nations publication, Sales No. 64.II.G.6), Richard Weisskoff, "Income Distribution and Economic Growth in Puerto Rico, Argentina, and Mexico," Review of Income and Wealth, December, 1970.
[a] Upper 20 percent of families.

Population and Income Size in Developing Countries

Market size may first be approximated by the size of population.[12] Most developing countries, however, have less than 5 million people; from a sample of 101 developing countries (with the combined population constituting about 99 percent of the figure for the whole developing economies), it appears that 73 countries have less than 10 million people:

DEVELOPING COUNTRIES: POPULATION DISTRIBUTION BY SIZE AND REGION, 1969

Population (in million)	Number of Countries			
	Africa	Asia	Western Hemisphere	Total
Over 50.0	1	3	1	5
20.1-50.0	2	5	3	10
10.1-20.0	6	6	1	13
5.1-10.0	8	5	3	16
4.1- 5.0	4	0	3	7
3.1- 4.0	7	1	2	10
2.1- 3.0	3	4	3	10
1.1- 2.0	5	2	4	11
1.0 and less	8	5	6	19

The majority of the least developed countries have a small population, in the range of 5 million or less.

As has been noted earlier, there are remarkable variations in per capita GNP among the developing countries. Some countries with relatively large populations have comparatively high per capita GNP (Brazil, Mexico), while other large countries have lower per capita figures (India, Indonesia). Many, however, have small population as well as low per capita GNP, yielding low absolute figures for their total GNP. In fact, the majority of the 101 develop-

ing countries included in the sample (where their combined GNP amounts to about 92 percent of the total figure
for the whole developing countries) have generated less
than $1 billion GNP; from the 55 countries that belong to
this group, 24 are listed as least developed:

**DEVELOPING COUNTRIES: GNP DISTRIBUTION
BY SIZE AND REGION, 1969**

| GNP (in billion dollars) | Number of Countries | | | |
	Africa	Asia	Western Hemisphere	Total
Over 30.0	0	1	0	1
20.1-30.0	0	0	2	2
15.1-20.0	0	1	1	2
10.1-15.0	0	1	0	1
5.1-10.0	2	4	3	9
4.1- 5.0	0	1	1	2
3.1- 4.0	1	3	0	4
2.1- 3.0	2	4	0	6
1.1- 2.0	9	6	4	19
1.0 and less	30	10	15	55

Partly in order to overcome the problems arising from
the small size of the market, regional economic groupings
have sprung up in the developing countries[13], some featur-
ing explicit schemes for industrial integration systems[14]. As
examples of these regional groupings it may be mentioned
that in Africa there are the East African Community
(EAC: Kenya, Tanzania, and Uganda) and the Central
African Customs and Economic Union (UDEAC: Cameroon, Central African Republic, Gabon, and the People's
Republic of the Congo); in Asia, Regional Cooperation for
Development (RCD: Iran, Pakistan, and Turkey) and Association of Southeast Asian Nations (ASEAN: Indonesia,
Malaysia, Philippines, Singapore, and Thailand); in Latin

America, the ANDEAN Group (Bolivia, Colombia, Chile, Ecuador, and Peru), the Central American Common Market (CACM: Costa Rica, El Salvador, Guatemala, Honduras, and Nicaragua), the Caribbean Free Trade Association (CARIFTA: Antigua, Barbados, Dominica, Grenada, Guyana, Jamaica, St. Kitts-Nevis-Anguilla, St. Lucia, Montserrat, Trinidad and Tobago, and St. Vincent), and the Latin American Free Trade Association (LAFTA: Argentina, Bolivia, Brazil, Colombia, Chile, Ecuador, Mexico, Paraguay, Peru, Uruguay, and Venezuela). The combined GNP of each of the regional economic groupings range in values from less than $2 billion to over $112 billion; the combined population and GNP figures for selected groupings are presented in the following table:

SELECTED REGIONAL ECONOMIC GROUPINGS:
POPULATION AND GNP, 1968

Economic Groupings	Population (in million)	GNP (in billion dollars)	Per Capita GNP (in dollars)
Africa:			
EAC	31	3.0	96
UDEAC	8	1.4	163
Asia:			
RCD	171	35.2	204
ASEAN	195	29.0	144
Western Hemisphere:			
ANDEAN	57	18.4	322
CACM	14	4.5	322
LAFTA	231	112.4	486

World Exports and the Developing Countries

It may be expected that the importance of foreign trade increases as the size of population decreases since the smaller countries may have relatively fewer resources, smaller market size, and less opportunities for internal trading relations as well as for self-sufficiency. Hence the ratio of exports to GNP might vary inversely with the size of population.

The expected pattern, however, is more pronounced in the developed countries. In the developing countries, the importance of exports in GNP depends more on the historical accident of the trade links between the export markets and the exporting countries. The destination of the bulk of exports in many developing countries is at most 3 or 4 developed countries. In 46 countries, one single agricultural or mineral product accounts for more than 40 percent of exports (19 countries dependent on single mineral, 27 on single agricultural commodity).

Although in the more populated developing economies exports as a percentage of GNP are relatively low, they vary considerably in the less populated countries (ranging from greater than 90 percent in Netherlands Antilles and Hong Kong to less than 5 percent in Laos and Mali). In general, the importance of exports in the developing economies with small population size seems to depend on the nature of their natural resources (with the exception of Hong Kong and Singapore).

The following figures illustrate the role of exports in the developing countries. Exports as a percentage of GNP in the 15 countries that have larger than 20 million people are in general lower than 10 percent. The Philippines, Thailand, and the United Arab Republic are exceptions, but the figures there are still within the 11 to 13 percent range. Iran, on the other hand, is also an exception due to its position as a major oil exporting country.

Among the 30 countries with 5 to 20 million people, the figures are in general greater than 15 percent, reaching as high as 25 percent in Tanzania and Uganda. Exceptions are observed in Afghanistan, Khmer Republic, Republic of Vietnam, Upper Volta, and Yemen Arab Republic where the figures are less than 10 percent. In petroleum and copper exporting countries, the figures are greater than 30 percent, nearing 90 percent in Saudi Arabia.

For the remaining 56 developing countries with less than 5 million population, the figures vary considerably. In 25 countries (9 of which are dependent on exports of petroleum products, copper, iron ore and concentrates, bauxite and aluminum, and precious stones), the figures are greater than 25 percent, reaching as high as 240 percent in the Netherlands Antilles. In 17 countries (11 of which are least developed), however, the figures are less than 15 percent.

In terms of world exports, by 1969 exports from the developing economies amounted to about 18 percent of the world total (the latter included Asian centrally planned economies, but excluded the trade of the People's Republic of China, Mongolia, North Korea, and North Vietnam with one another). Around 30 percent of the developing countries exports were accounted for by fuels and related materials. During 1950-68, the average annual rate of growth of exports of the developing countries (about 5 percent) lagged behind the rates of growth of both the centrally planned and the developed market economies (around 8 to 9 percent). Accordingly, the share of exports of the developing countries in the world total exhibited a declining trend:

**WORLD EXPORTS PERCENTAGE DISTRIBUTION
BY MAJOR ECONOMIC GROUPINGS**

Category	Percentage shares		
	1950	1960	1969
World economy	100.0	100.0	100.0
Developed economies	60.8	67.0	71.2
Developing economies	31.2	21.3	17.9
Centrally planned economies	8.0	11.7	10.9

Sources: Review of International Trade and Development, 1970, and Handbook of International Trade and Development Statistics, Supplement 1970.

While intratrade among the developed countries has continued to expand, in the developing economies during 1960-69 the shares of intratrade to their total exports declined from 22 to 20 percent. Exports from the developed to the developing countries as percentage of the former total exports declined from over 25 percent in 1960 to less than 20 percent in 1969. It appears that the developing countries as a group have become less and less important in the world market, while at the same time they are trading less (in relative terms) among themselves: during 1960-67, while total exports grew at an annual rate of 6.3 percent, intratrade grew at 4.2 percent.

The commodities which the developing countries are able to export show declining importance in total world trade. During 1955-68, the share of manufactured goods in total world exports increased from 50 to 64 percent; the share of the primary commodities, on the other hand, fell, where the largest decline is observed in food, beverages, and raw materials (from 39 to 26 percent):

COMMODITY STRUCTURE OF WORLD EXPORTS

Commodity Class	Percentage shares		
	1955	1960	1968
Food and beverages	19.0	17.6	14.5
Raw materials	19.0	16.9	11.6
Fuels	11.2	10.0	9.8
Chemicals	5.1	5.9	7.2
Machineries and transport equipment	18.4	22.0	27.9
Other manufactures	26.3	27.6	29.0
Primary commodities	50.2	44.5	35.9
Manufactured goods	49.8	55.5	64.1

Source: Handbook of International Trade and Development Statistics, Supplement 1970.

While primary commodities account for nearly nine-tenths of the total exports from the developing countries, the latter only amount to less than one-half of the world's total. The largest component by far is petroleum and related products, originating mostly from the principal sources: the Caribbean, Iran, Iraq, Kuwait, Libya, Saudi Arabia, and Venezuela; it may be noted, however, that about one-third of the world's oil comes principally from the U.S. and the U.S.S.R. Second in importance is coffee, where more than half of the world's exports have originated from Brazil, Colombia, Ivory Coast, and Uganda.

The third is copper, from two principal sources (Chile and Zambia); half of the world's copper, on the other hand, is mined in Canada and the United States. Fourth is sugar, followed by cotton (the world's largest producers of cotton are the U.S. and the U.S.S.R.); vegetable oils and fats (about one-third of vegetable oils exports is from the U.S. alone); rubber, iron ore, tin, etc. Thus, even among the primary commodities, there are many in which the nondeveloping countries are able to compete, either through direct production or through the production of substitutes.

It may also be noted that there are asymmetrical trade relations between the developed and the developing countries. The developed economies are not heavily dependent on the developing countries; by contrast, the developing economies are highly dependent on the developed countries for their exports, while at the same time their markets are relatively not well dispersed.

About one-third of the exports from Latin America and the Caribbean goes to Canada and the U.S., while another third goes to Western Europe; nearly two-thirds of West African exports are sent to Western Europe and Japan; slightly over three-fourths of Northern African exports are sent to Western Europe; about one-fifth of East Asian exports go to Japan and another two-fifths to other developed countries. On the other hand, only about one-sixth of the exports from Australia, New Zealand, and South Africa goes to the developing countries; one-fifth of the exports of Western Europe (about evenly distributed throughout the various regions) goes to the developing societies. One-fourth of the exports from Canada and the United States and two-fifths of the exports from Japan go to the developing countries.

In most developing countries manufacturing exports are insignificant: in more than half the 88 countries sampled, the shares of exports of manufactures amount to at most 5 percent of the total value of exports. In fact, in 50 developing countries per capita exports of manufactured goods is less than $1, exceeding $10 in only about 7 countries. The range of manufacturing exports from the developing countries is quite narrowly diversified; about half is textiles and clothing.

DEVELOPING COUNTRIES: PERCENTAGE DISTRIBUTION OF THE SHARES OF MANUFACTURES IN TOTAL EXPORTS, AROUND 1968

Share of Manufactures	Number of developing countries
Under 1.1	19
1.1-5.0	26
5.1-10.0	16
10.1-20.0	14
20.1-50.0	7
Over 50.0	6

Source: Handbook of International Trade and Development Statistics, Supplement 1970.

It should be emphasized, however, that the figures do not indicate the import-content of the manufacturing exports, nor the fact that in some cases these exports are being produced by industries which are owned and controlled by foreign corporations or their affiliates. In cases where foreign control and ownership are dominant, and where the import-content is high, the effect of the upsurge in manufacturing exports may only take the form of high wages; if this upsurge is limited to the intratrade within a regional economic grouping and has been facilitated only by high protective tariff, the effect is at once lessened because the consumers have to pay higher prices (in effect the nationals are subsidizing the foreign companies).

Thus, it can be mentioned, for example, that among the members of the Central American Common Market there was an impressive expansion of intraregional trade in manufactured goods due among other factors to high regional protective tariffs offered to finished goods and low tariffs for raw materials and intermediate products. By 1968, in each member country manufacturing exports ranged from 12 percent of total exports in Nicaragua to 19 percent in Costa Rica. It has been argued, however, that this was achieved at considerable economic (and social) cost to the region.[15] Among the economic costs are the rapidly growing import bill (due to the high import-content of the manufactured goods) to the countries outside the region, a decline in fiscal revenues (from the loss of import duties), high prices to the consumers for the protected manufactured goods, and the exorbitant profits accruing mainly to foreign-owned manufacturing industries.

Industrial Origin of GDP

The somewhat insignificant manufacturing exports in many developing countries and the lack of their export diversification are related, to a certain extent, to the economic structure of these countries. Although the contribution of the manufacturing sector can exceed 30 percent in very few countries (Argentina, Singapore), in 37 other developing countries it is less than 10 percent. The following table indicates that from a sample of 87 developing countries, 76 indicate that the manufacturing sector contributes only 20 percent or less in generating GDP:

**DEVELOPING COUNTRIES: DISTRIBUTION
OF PERCENTAGE SHARE OF MANUFACTURING
SECTOR IN GDP, AROUND 1967**

Share of manufacturing	Number of countries			
	Africa	Asia	Western Hemisphere	Total
Over 50	0	1	0	1
31-50	0	0	1	1
21-30	1	3	5	9
11-20	11	12	16	39
Under 11	29	7	1	37

Sources: Yearbook of National Accounts Statistics, Vol. II, 1969; Review of
International Trade and Development, 1970; Handbook of International Trade
and Development Statistics, Supplement 1970.

The World Bank has suggested that it will be convenient to classify the developing countries in accordance with their levels of industrial development; one approximate measure of the latter is the proportion of gross value added in manufacturing to gross value added in commodity production (where commodities are taken to mean the productions of agriculture, mining, and manufacturing, and of abilities producing power, gas, and water). Thus, countries with less than 20 percent manufacturing in total commodity production are defined as *nonindustrial*; those between 20 and 40 percent are considered as *industrializing*; those between 40 and 60 percent as *semiindustrialized*; those with greater than 60 percent as *industrialized*. From a sample of 82 developing countries based on the data for 1968, it appears that 34 are characterized as nonindustrial; 35 industrializing; 11 semiindustrialized; and 2 industrialized developing countries.

It may be noted that an adjustment has been made for large countries such as India, Nigeria, and Pakistan, where the internal market is considered large enough for industry to be relatively developed although its contribution to the total commodity production is still low. On the other

**DEVELOPING COUNTRIES ACCORDING TO THEIR
LEVELS OF INDUSTRIAL DEVELOPMENT, 1968**

Levels of Industrialization	Number of countries			
	Africa	Asia	Western Hemisphere	Total
Nonindustrial	28	5	1	34
Industrializing	10	10	15	35
Semiindustrialized	1	4	6	11
Industrialized	0	2	0	2

Source: Industry, Sector Working Paper, World Bank pamphlet, April, 1972.

hand, in certain other countries, e.g., Argentina, Israel, and
Mexico, the relatively high estimates for the proportion of
manufacturing reflect in part the effects of protection in
rising prices in the manufacturing sector.

In some, the low level of manufacturing is compen-
sated by a high industrial activity related to mineral extrac-
tion (Algeria, Liberia, Libya, Mauritania, Zambia), so that
agriculture is not dominant in GDP. In over 30 other
developing countries, however, agriculture generates more
than 40 percent of GDP:

**DEVELOPING COUNTRIES: DISTRIBUTION OF
PERCENTAGE SHARES OF AGRICULTURE IN GDP
AROUND 1967**

Shares of Agriculture	Number of countries			
	Africa	Asia	Western Hemisphere	Total
Over 50	15	2	0	17
41-50	6	6	2	14
26-40	9	6	10	25
11-25	5	6	9	20
10 and below	2	1	3	6

It may be noted that the comparable figure for Japan
during the early phase of its development was 64 percent
for the years 1878-82, according to the estimate of
Ohkawa and Rosovsky.[16]

In many predominantly agricultural developing countries, the low level of manufacturing is also accompanied
by a low literacy rate. It might be expected that countries
with a low literacy rate are in a relatively disadvantaged
position in providing skilled manpower for the manufacturing industries, although illiteracy as such does not
necessarily present an insurmountable barrier for the development of the manufacturing sector (as exemplified by
experiences in the Soviet Union[17] and the People's Republic of China[18]), nor does a high literacy rate eliminate the
bottlenecks for industrialization (in Ceylon and Costa Rica
the rates are 75 and 84 percent, respectively, and in many
developing countries there are phenomena of educated
unemployment).

In Table I-1 of the Appendix the shares of manufacturing, industrial, and agricultural sectors in GDP are presented for 47 developing countries, while Table I-2 of the
Appendix shows the relationship of sectoral outputs per
economically active population. The countries chosen for
the sample are those which show either low manufacturing share (10 percent of GDP or less), or low literacy
rate (where the proportion of the population fifteen
years or over that are literate is 20 percent or less), or
both.

It can be seen from Table I-1 that in most low-manufacturing developing countries, more than four-fifths of
the economically active population are in agriculture.
According to the estimate of Kiga[18], about 82 percent of
all people employed in Japan worked in the agricultural
sector in 1880.

Although agriculture is dominant in generating GDP,
its output proportion is not commensurate with the high
percentage of the economically active population to be

found in this sector, pointing out to a wide productivity gap between agriculture and other sectors. In fact, output per economically active population in agriculture is considerably less than that of other sectors. In most countries, gross value added per economically active population in the nonagricultural sector is at least four times the corresponding figure in agriculture; in 12 countries it reaches ten to twenty times higher:

SELECTED DEVELOPING COUNTRIES: RATIOS OF GROSS VALUE ADDED IN AGRICULTURE TO GROSS VALUE ADDED IN NONAGRICULTURAL SECTORS, PER ECONOMICALLY ACTIVE POPULATION IN THE RESPECTIVE SECTORS, AROUND 1967

Ratios in percent	Number of developing countries
1-5	4
6-10	8
11-15	6
16-20	7
21-25	2
26-40	3
Over 40	4

Source: Table I-2.

It may be noted that in the developed countries the ratios range from 50 to 80 percent.

The ratios, obviously, merely measure the discrepancies of sectoral outputs per economically active population. The data, however, also suggest that in general productivity in agriculture is low. In most of the developing countries sampled, gross value added per economically active population in agriculture is $200 or less; in 9 countries, the figures are $100 or less, reaching as low as $40 in Zaire:

SELECTED DEVELOPING COUNTRIES: DISTRIBUTION
OF GROSS VALUE ADDED PER ECONOMICALLY ACTIVE
POPULATION IN AGRICULTURE, AROUND 1967

Amount in dollars	Number of developing countries
Under 50	1
51-100	8
101-150	6
151-200	6
Over 200	12

Source: Table I-2.

In 18 of the developing countries sampled, the figures
are more than $1,000:

SELECTED DEVELOPING COUNTRIES: DISTRIBUTION
OF GROSS VALUE ADDED PER ECONOMICALLY ACTIVE
POPULATION IN NON-AGRUCULTURE, AROUND 1967

Amount in dollars	Number of developing countries
301-500	3
501-1000	12
1001-2000	12
2001-4000	2
Over 4000	4

Source: Table I-2.

Notwithstanding the relatively high productivity in the
nonagricultural sector, since agriculture in many of these
countries is dominant, output per economically active
population in all sectors (including agriculture) in the
majority of these countries (22 of them) is at most twice
the corresponding figure in agriculture:

SELECTED DEVELOPING COUNTRIES: RATIO OF
GROSS VALUE ADDED IN AGRICULTURE TO GROSS
VALUE ADDED IN ALL SECTORS PER ECONOMICALLY
ACTIVE POPULATION IN ALL SECTORS, AROUND 1967

Ratios in percent	Number of developing countries
10-20	2
21-30	2
31-40	2
41-50	5
51-60	8
61-80	13
Over 80	1

Source: Table I-2.

Accordingly, gross value added per economically active
population in most countries is at most $400; in 13
countries it is $200 or less (reaching as low as $90 in
Upper Volta):

SELECTED DEVELOPING COUNTRIES: DISTRIBUTION OF
GROSS VALUE ADDED PER ECONOMICALLY ACTIVE
POPULATION IN ALL SECTORS, AROUND 1967

Amount in dollars	Number of developing countries
51-100	1
101-150	2
151-200	10
201-250	5
251-300	2
301-400	7
Over 400	12

Source: Table I-2.

An obvious fact which may be emphasized is that in
these predominantly agricultural-oriented developing countries, the growth rate in GDP cannot be very much higher
than the growth rate of agricultural production due to the
latter's sheer weight.

Growth in GDP and some of Its Components

For the whole developing countries, preliminary estimates indicate that the rate of growth of GDP in the first
year of the United Nations Second Development Decade is
5.4 percent, somewhat lower than the target rate of 6
percent but as good as the average performance in the First
Decade.

DEVELOPING COUNTRIES: PERCENT RATIO OF GROWTH IN GDP AT CONSTANT MARKET PRICES, 1961-1971

AVERAGE ANNUAL RATES

Regional Grouping	1955-1960[a]	1961-1970	Change from the preceding Year 1971
Developing Countries			
Total	4.6	5.1	5.4
Africa	4.3	4.4	4.5
Other Asia	4.2	4.9	4.5
West Asia	6.5	7.6	7.7
Western Hemisphere	4.6	5.2	6.5

Source: World Economic Survey, 1971 (United Nations Publication, Sales
No. E.72.II.C.2) and earlier issue.
[a]at constant factor cost.

During the first year of the Second Development
Decade, 34 of the 83 developing countries sampled indicate
that their growth rates are larger than the target rate; in

this respect, the number of developing countries is greater as compared to that observed in the First Decade. If the growth rates that are higher than 6.0 percent are described as *high-growth*, between 4.0 and 6.0 percent as *medium-growth*, and those lower than 4.0 percent as *low-growth*, then during 1960-68 there were 22 high-growth developing countries, 34 medium-growth and 33 low-growth. (Low-growth has occurred mostly in nonindustrial developing countries; medium- and high-growth mostly in countries at higher stages of industrialization.)

Two-thirds of the low-growth developing countries are nonindustrial, while 3 countries (Argentina, India, and Uruguay) are at a semiindustrial stage. On the other hand, more than half of medium-growth countries are at the stage of industrializing and one-fourth are nonindustrial. Less than one-third of the high-growth countries are nonindustrial; these countries are Gambia, Ivory Coast, Lesotho, Mauritania, Togo, and Zambia. (It may be noted, however, that the growth rates in per capita GNP during the same period for Gambia, Lesotho, and Togo merely range from zero to less than 1 percent.)

DEVELOPING COUNTRIES: ANNUAL PERCENTAGE GDP GROWTH RATES IN REAL TERMS (1960-68) POPULATION DISTRIBUTION (1968) AND LEVELS OF INDUSTRIAL DEVELOPMENT (1968)

Category of GDP growth rates	Population in percent of total sampled	Number of Countries			
		Non-industrial	Indus-trializing	Semi-indus-trialized	Indus-trialized
High-growth	11.1	6	9	4	1
Medium-growth	28.9	8	18	4	1
Low-growth	60.0	20	8	3	0

Sources: World Economic Survey, 1970; Review of International Trade and Development, 1970; Monthly Bulletin of Statistics.

Note: The countries included in the sample are restricted to those wherein the corresponding data on the level of industrial development are available.

Of the 22 high-growth developing countries, only about one-fourth are countries with per capita GDP lower than the developing countries average (Gambia, Lesotho, Mauritania, Republic of Korea, Thailand, and Togo) and 5 countries are endowed with rich mineral resources (oil in Iran, Libya, and Saudi Arabia; copper in Zambia; iron ore in Mauritania). Of the 34 medium-growth countries less than one-fourth have lower than average per capita GDP (Bolivia, Botswana, Ceylon, Ethiopia, Guinea, Kenya, Niger, and Pakistan); on the other hand, of the 33 low-growth countries less than one-fourth are those with higher than average per capita GDP (Algeria, Argentina, Dominican Republic, Ghana, Guyana, People's Republic of Congo, Senegal, and Uruguay). Thus, countries with lower than average per capita GDP account for more than three-fourths of the low-growth developing countries and less than one-fourth of those with medium- and high-growth rates. Higher- and medium-growth rates have occurred mostly in the richer and the more industrialized developing countries, while the low-growth rates occurred in the poorer and the less industrialized but with the population majority.

In terms of the annual growth rates in per capita GNP during 1960-69, the general picture obtained above is not substantially altered. Out of the 87 developing countries sampled, 51 (six-tenths of which have lower than average per capita GDP, accounting for about three-fourths of the population in the developing countries) achieved at most 2 percent annual growth in their per capita GNP; in 30 of these countries (two-thirds of which have lower than average per capita GDP, amounting to about one-fifth of population) the growth in GNP barely kept up with the growth of population.

The 7 countries with lower than average per capita GDP but which have managed to obtain greater than 2 percent growth rates in their per capita GNP are (figures in brackets indicate the growth rates): Bolivia (2.4), Ethiopia (2.3), Gambia (2.6), Korea (6.4), Mauritania (4.6),

DEVELOPING COUNTRIES: AVERAGE ANNUAL PERCENTAGE
GROWTH RATES OF PER CAPITA GNP IN REAL TERMS
(1960-69) AND POPULATION DISTRIBUTION (1968)

| | | Number of Countries | |
Growth rates	Population in percent of total sampled	Total	Those with lower than the developing countries average per capita GDP
Smaller than			
0.0	6.2	9	4
0.0-1.0	14.2	21	16
1.1-2.0	53.9	21	11
2.1-3.0	12.9	17	4
3.1-5.0	9.8	13	2
Greater than			
5.0	3.2	6	1

Source: World Bank Atlas; Monthly Bulletin of Statistics.

Pakistan (2.9), and Thailand (4.7), 3 of which are at the nonindustrial stages.

It has been noted earlier that many developing countries are predominantly agricultural, so that their growth rates in GDP cannot be very much higher than their growth rates in agricultural production. Throughout 1960-68, the average annual rate of increase in the gross agricultural production index for the whole developing countries (for which data are available) according to USDA figures was 2.5 percent. However, it does not appear that the nonindustrial developing countries have performed well, although it must be emphasized that data coverage for these countries is very limited (only 23 out of 34 nonindustrial developing countries).

From a sample of 66 developing countries, 30 indicate higher than average annual increase in gross agricultural

production; only 6 of these countries are nonindustrial
(Iraq, Ivory Coast, Sudan, Tanzania, Uganda, and Zambia),
while 18 are industrializing and the remaining 6 semiindustrialized. In fact, from the 16 developing countries that
have obtained average annual rates of increase in excess of
4 percent, only Zambia is nonindustrial. Most nonindustrial developing countries have performed worse than
average, while most of the industrializing and semiindustrialized countries better than average:

DEVELOPING COUNTRIES: AVERAGE ANNUAL RATES OF INCREASE IN GROSS AGRICULTURAL PRODUCTION INDEX 1960-68 AND LEVELS OF INDUSTRIAL DEVELOPMENT (1968)

Rates of increase in percent	Number of developing countries		
	Nonindustrial	Industrializing	Semiindustrialized
Lower than 0.0	1	2	0
0.0-1.0	3	8	2
1.1-2.5	13	4	3
2.6-4.0	5	7	2
Greater than 4.0	1	11	4

Source: World Economic Survey, 1970.

In food production the situation is somewhat similar:
from the 31 countries that have performed better than the
average of 2.6 percent for the whole developing countries,
only 5 (Iraq, Ivory Coast, Malawi, Tanzania, and Zambia)
are nonindustrial, while 19 are industrializing and the
remaining 6 semiindustrial. Figures for the average annual
rates of increase in 4 nonindustrial developing countries
(Algeria, Haiti, Mali, and Zaire) are even negative. Again,
most nonindustrial developing countries included in the
sample performed worse than average, while most industrializing and semiindustrialized developing countries performed better than average:

DEVELOPING COUNTRIES: AVERAGE ANNUAL RATES OF
INCREASE IN GROSS FOOD PRODUCTION INDEX (1960-68)
AND LEVELS OF INDUSTRIAL DEVELOPMENT (1968)

Rates of increase in percent	Number of developing countries		
	Nonindustrial	Industrializing	Semiindustrialized
Lower than 0.0	4	4	0
0.0-1.0	2	8	1
1.1-2.5	12	1	3
2.6-4.0	2	7	2
Greater than 4.0	3	12	5

Source: World Economic Survey, 1970.

The data coverage for the average annual rates of
growth of real gross value added in manufacturing throughout 1960-69 for the nonindustrial developing countries is
even more limited (available in only 17 out of the 34
countries). Out of these 17 countries, only 4 achieved rates
of growth between 15 and 20 percent (Algeria, Tanzania,
Upper Volta, and Zambia) and 7 between 10 and 20
percent (with the addition of Ivory Coast, Sudan, and
Togo):

DEVELOPING COUNTRIES: AVERAGE ANNUAL RATES OF GROWTH
OF REAL GROSS VALUE ADDED IN MANUFACTURING (1960-69)
AND LEVELS OF INDUSTRIAL DEVELOPMENT

Rates of Growth	Number of countries			
	Nonindus- trializing	Indus- trializing	Semiindus- trialized	Indus- trialized
0-5.0	5	12	2	0
5.1-10.0	5	10	3	0
10.1-15.0	3	10	1	1
15.1-20.0	4	10	0	1

Source: Industry, World Bank pamphlet, April, 1972.

Diverging Initial Conditions and
Development Problems

The preceding discussions attempt to show that even within the confines of a limited number of observed variables, it is too far-fetched to suggest that the developing countries are characterized by uniformity or homogeneity. Although in some 50 developing countries (populated by about 1.2 billion people) per capita income is lower than $200, in over 15 others it is more than $500; while in about 55 countries total GNP is lower than $1 billion, in 5 others it is more than $10 billion. Similarly, population in about 60 countries is less than 5 million and in 5 others it is larger than 50 million.

The broad structure of production also indicates considerable diversity. On the one hand, over 30 countries are predominantly agricultural and at the nonindustrial stage, while on the other, some have lower than 10 percent agricultural share in GDP; there are also the so-called industrialized developing countries. Even the countries with somewhat similar manufacturing shares in GDP are grouped together. There is a diversity observed in the figures for sectoral outputs per economically active population. The importance and structure of exports are also varied, not necessarily correlated with the size of population.

Given such a diversity, generalization regarding the universal state of underdevelopment is somewhat tenuous. Upon examining the growth rates of GDP, agricultural, food, and manufacturing production, however, it appears that broad generalities (although subject to exceptions as applied to individual countries) regarding their patterns of growth are inescapable—that higher growth rates in the respective variables have occurred mostly in the richer developing countries and/or those at the higher stages of industrialization.

The data enumeration above, and observations suggested, therefore, are of course superficial by nature. They merely relate to those directly discernible from the given observed data without probing into the deeper question of why the data behave as they do; thus, for example, there is no attempt at an explanation of why certain developing countries are relatively richer than others, nor why they have managed to reach a higher stage of development and to obtain higher rates of growth. The nature of development policies being pursued, the institutional setting, the political and social frameworks that directly or indirectly affect economic variables are not examined. The meaning and interpretation of the data presented are not considered.

An important question related to the problem of interpretation is the question of the ownership and control of the means of production which directly affects the distribution of income. In many developing countries, the dynamic industries (and modernized agriculture) are often owned and controlled by foreign nationals or foreign corporations, or by an oligarchy of indigenous and non-indigenous nationals. The mass of the indigenous population (even after independence) are mainly confined to stagnant low-productivity agriculture. On the other hand, the locus of power structure in many developing countries is substantially affected by a dynamic complex of linkages between economic strength and the control of decision making. The majority of the populace in the relatively richer and dynamically growing developing countries is not necessarily better-off than that in the apparently poorer and stagnant countries.

Even such superficial enumeration, however, is quite revealing. Any theory of economic development that does not take into account such divergent conditions existing within the developing countries can be questioned with regard to its relevance and its realism, unless it can be shown that such divergent conditions are irrelevant. Too often a theory is built on this simplistic notion by incorporating certain specific characteristics of some type of developing countries and then proceeding therefrom with a sweeping generalization for all developing countries.

There have been theories of economic development specifically designed for the developing countries that do not appear to stand the test of relevance and realism. For example, in the 1950s the theories of "vicious circle," "take-off," and "big push" were very popular. These theories contain inherent weaknesses by trying to apply a composite model of the developing countries, incorporating certain special features of some types of a developing country, to all developing countries. The "vicious circle" presumes low income in the form of a general state of poverty and stagnation (note the diverging income figures and their rates of growth); the "take-off" (which, after all, is a mere summary of the European experience) assumes the preexistence of a fairly high level of development in the political, social, and institutional framework; the "big push" assumes both as well as a sufficiently large internal market to support a domestic capital goods sector. By the time all these special features have been incorporated into a composite model of development, the number of developing countries for which this model might apply will be reduced to 1 or 2 countries.[19]

With the increasing usage of mathematical and econometric tools, it has become fashionable to construct growth models (and models of economic development), based on intertemporal and intercountry analyses. The act of theorizing is to be able to simplify complex phenomena of real events into a simple system of understandable thoughts which facilitate meaningful insights; such a theory is useful if it assists in the making of the best decision. In this respect mathematical and econometric tools are helpful and powerful devices permitting rigorous tests of the logical consistency and empirical validity of a system of thought, based on objective and universally applicable laws of transformation. The danger lies in the fact that sometimes prior simplifications are made in order to permit the formulation of a hypothesis, but these subsequently general prescriptions based on such hypothesies are considered to be universally applicable to all developing countries.

Dynamic economic theory in the form of growth models are not very relevant and are not meant to be relevant for the developing countries.[20] The wrong choice of theoretical models to be applied to the developing countries is an important cause for the lack of realism; the greatest mistake is to succumb to the lure of the "intellectual steel mills"[21] represented by the latest and most sophisticated theoretical gadgets, and to allow oneself to be in the grip of alien ideas based on substantially irrelevant experience.

Patterns of economic development obtained from intercountry econometric analysis may show the broad picture of the interrelationship between development variables. The analysis, however, tends to regard each country included in the sample as a mere dot in the scatter diagram, disregarding the fact that there are complex factors at work which place a country on such a particular dot.

It may be useful to distinguish the *theory* of development from the *process* of development.[22] The process of development is an integral part consisting of three highly interrelated elements: the initial conditions; the mechanism for economic development; and the strategy and policy being adopted.

The theory of economic development, on the other hand, is but one of the aspects describing the mechanism for economic development, the latter covering the formulation of behaviorial patterns, objective laws of transformation governing physical and technical relationships among the variables, and equilibrium condition such that the interaction between the behaviorial patterns and the laws of transformation results in an economic growth.

If the initial conditions, as well as the policy and strategy being adopted, could all be taken as predetermined variables and data which need not be analyzed further, the distinction loses much of its significance: the mechanism for economic development would suffice to describe the process under the given assumption. However, since even at the superficial level, diversity among the contemporary developing countries could be discerned, it is questionable whether such an assumption is valid.

Much of the thinking and writing on economic development (in market and centrally planned economies alike) have utilized as a frame of reference the economic, political, social, and institutional backgrounds of the developed countries, combined with the general temptation to extrapolate the development problems and prospects of contemporary developing countries from the earlier growth patterns of these developed countries (at their presumed similar state of underdevelopment). Simon Kuznets has stressed certain basic characteristics of the developing countries, pointing up the differences between them and the comparable characteristics of the presently developed countries during the decades preceding their industrialization, in order to obtain a more realistic appraisal of the magnitude and recalcitrance of the problems of economic development; these differences are considered as obstacles to such extrapolation.[23]

Contrasting the present problems of economic development with the experiences of the presently advanced but formerly developing countries will probably reduce itself to the case of Japan[24] since the Meiji Restoration. Shigeru Ishicawa[25], on the other hand, has elaborated further on Kuznets' analysis while at the same time examining the problems of what was, after all, the Japanese experience, and whether its experience is relevant as a lesson to the contemporary developing countries in Asia.

According to Kuznets, there are seven characteristics which constitute obstacles to economic growth that are "more formidable than may have been the case in the presently developed countries in their pre-industrial phase."[26] *First*, the present levels of per capita product in the developing countries are much lower than those in Western and central Europe, North Amercia, and Oceania during their preindustrialization phase: even at 1952-54 prices, the figures for the latter ranged well above $200 (in the Soviet Union, per capita income around 1885 was probably more than $150). *Second*, in contemporary developing countries, there is now a much lower supply of agricultural land per capita (and per agricultural worker also). *Third*, indirect evidence strongly suggests the lower productivity of the agricultural sector (per worker income in this sector must be one-fourth to one-third of per worker income in agriculture in the currently developed countries in their preindustrialization phase).

Fourth, irregularity in the size distribution of income may be wider or it is at best as wide. *Fifth*, social and political concomitants of the low income structure appear to constitute more formidable obstacles to economic growth. (Birth rates in the preindustrialization phase were as high as those in the presently developing countries only when the ratio of population to resources was extremely favorable; the literacy rates in the presently developing countries are probably well below although more important in their cultural and linguistic diversity; weak political structure in the developing countries, characterized by the cleavage between the masses of population struggling for a meagre subsistence and the smaller groups of elites, easily leads to dictatorial or oligarchial regimes which are often unstable and most unresponsive to the basic problems of their country.)

Sixth, after decades of either colonial status or political inferiority, most developing countries have attained political independence only recently (in contrast to the advanced countries where industrialization followed a long period of political independence). *Seventh*, the presently developed countries within the European orbit are inheritors of European civilization, which, through centuries of geographical, political, moral, and intellectual revolutions that occurred within the context of their own civilization, has produced the matrix of modern economic growth; participation in the long process of change prior to the

emergence of the industrial system meant gradual adaptation, an opportunity to develop within the existing social
and political frameworks the new institutions necessary to
exploit the potentials provided by these revolutions. By
the time these countries reached their preindustrialization
phase, they already possessed a variety of social, political,
and economic institutions that facilitated the further
adjustment which industrialization brought in its wake or
which were the essential concomitants (in contrast to the
developing countries, very often inheritors of alien civiliza-
tions imposed with disruptive and sometimes painful
effects, which, though containing changes, are not the
matrix out of which modern economic growth has
emerged).

Although the list should suffice to convey the far-
reaching and striking differences, it is by no means exhaustive and has been admitted as such. References to the
social and political frameworks and the differences in
historical antecedents are no more than a few broad
strokes on a vast canvas; there are no references to the
division between participation and property incomes; the
savings and capital investment proportions; the spread of
the market economy and the availability of credit and
financial institutions; the fiscal and tax systems; the
dependence upon foreign trade.[27]

One thing which may be added, and emphasized, is
that the constellation of the nineteenth-century world
order is different from the twentieth century and this has a
pervasive influence on the pattern of development of the
contemporary developing countries.

Even apart from the unidirectional flow of economic
benefits from colonialization, which characterized the
nineteenth-century world order (whose contribution to the
economic development of the metropolitan power is not
to be underestimated), those countries without particularly rich natural resources could proceed with their
industrialization through relative technological superiority
and by taking advantage of foreign trade.

It may be briefly mentioned, for example, that the early expansion of the British industrial economy relied mainly on international trade (with the exception of coal, its domestic supplies of raw materials were not impressive; some crucial industries such as cotton depended entirely on imports).[28] Through technological supremacy and its virtual monopoly of industrialization, the United Kingdom engaged in a massive interchange whereby the rest of the world was initially transformed into a set of economies that were dependent on and complimentary to the British economy; these economies were, for example: Argentina (wheat, beef); Australia (wool); Chile (nitrates and copper); Denmark (dairy products); Portugal (wine); South Africa (gold and diamonds); the United States (cotton); and, not the least important, the colonies. It may also be noted that British dominance over the high seas preempted rival trading powers.

By contrast, the developing countries are characterized by technological and industrial inferiority and they have not much to offer in international trade beyond those commodities based on natural resources and local unskilled labor. Both of these are more and more subjected to technological obsolescence, resulting in a subordinate position in international trade relations and making them the weak victim of external vulnerability. Whatever manufactured exports they have to offer, the goods are very often faced with formidable trade obstacles in the developed countries. With the passage of time and technological progress, it is more likely that comparative advantage based substantially on natural resources and local unskilled labor will become more and more unimportant. The contemporary developing countries have to be content with the oligopolistic and monopsonistic world markets, which have considerable power and leverage.

Technological obsolescence does not only affect the developing countries in their world market position; it also affects the options available for their strategy and policy of economic development. Abundant unskilled labor involves social problems, but it has become increasingly difficult to provide productive employment for them. The productivity gap between the developed and the developing countries is so large and increasingly widening that efficiency consideration might force the adoption of modern techniques.

It may be argued that the known potential of modern technology is an advantage to the developing countries (where the problem could then be simplified into the question of the application of science and technology to the developing countries); it should be emphasized, however, that the modern technology being adopted in the advanced countries has evolved as a response to the needs of their economies and has been adapted to the pattern of factors availability peculiar to these countries. At one time or another, the range of tested knowledge and scientific discoveries at the disposal of the developed countries also exceeded the capacity for their utilization in production so that the mere fact that modern techniques are available to the developing countries is not necessarily a great advantage. The time span between the underlying scientific discoveries and their subsequent utilization in production was in general quite long: the known technological potential had to be adapted to the availability of capital, labor, and economic entrepreneurship.

The immediate transplanting of modern technology originating from the advanced countries carries the danger that its factor requirements could substantially differ from the factors availability in the developing countries. Thus, for example, modern technology is usually capital-intensive and labor-saving, while the developing countries are characterized by capital scarcity and abundant labor; in agriculture, in addition to these, technological innovations are usually not land-saving (while land is the more limiting factor of production in many developing countries). One of the difficult problems in formulating the strategy and policy for economic development is to ensure that input utilization is in consonance with the availability of the factors of production, but modern technology makes available abundant unskilled labor less and less relevant. The tendency is toward the divergence of factors utilization from factors availability; while crucially dependent on certain imported inputs, the developing countries are at the same time having idly unemployed domestic resources.

Different nations have relied upon different industries as the leading sectors at various periods of their industrialization process. It has been pointed out, however, that the industrialization process shows a rather uniform pattern in all the countries that have passed through it.[29] The traditional pattern of manufacturing development is to move from consumer goods to capital goods industries: at the earlier stage of industrial development, the ratio of the former to the latter is around 5:1, and finally it declines to 2:1 and even to less than 1:1.

Technological obsolescence (in conjunction with the difficulties encountered in exporting manufactured products), on the other hand, may make it necessary to have an inward-directed development strategy, where consumer, intermediate, and capital goods industries might have to be synchronized and developed simultaneously. Such inward-looking development strategy, however, will be facing formidable obstacles in the form of limited material and financial resources, technical and managerial skills, as well as the size of the domestic market. The technological gap will also give rise to the problem of to what extent the interest of consumers could and should be sacrificed in order to support an inward-looking development strategy or, for that matter, any efforts at industrialization. The infant-industry argument is probably more difficult to apply now than during the nineteenth-century world order. Many industries in the developing countries exist only because of enormously high protective tariffs, whose existence merely assumes a somewhat symbolic nature: these industries have a very high import-content (with little or no linkage effects to the domestic sector, notably assembling and finishing-touches industries which depend entirely on a few foreign manufacturers), making them vulnerable to external forces. It may be noted that the greater the import-content[30], the higher the burden to consumers.

The technological superiority of the advanced countries applies not only to the area of manufacturing industries but to agriculture as well: per hectare outputs of major food crops in the United States, for example, are higher than those in India. While it is not clear how agricultural progress preceded industrialization, agricultural output and productivity increased markedly during the initial phase of industrialization in the advanced countries.[31] With the exception of Britain, the advanced countries during their industrialization period were able to feed their own people and some were even major exporters of foodstuffs.

Many contemporary developing countries, on the other hand, are spending considerable amounts of scarce foreign exchange on imports of foodstuffs and agricultural products. In some instances these food imports are directly competitive with domestic production, permitting the formation of artificially low domestic prices (encouraging consumption and discouraging production), which may result in a perpetual state of food deficit. While high domestic prices for manufacturing goods are tolerated to promote and support industrialization, high domestic prices for foodstuffs are not generally palatable for they clash with the interest of the urban dwellers, who exert considerable political leverage. The Green Revolution is often considered as the panacea for offering a dramatic increase in agricultural productivity; it is, however, capital-intensive (with high import-content) and would lead to factors utilization, which could diverge considerably from factors availability, and tends to favor big landowners.

Another complicating factor is the extent of foreign influence in the domestic economy of the contemporary developing countries. The problem is of course not unique. As Hobsbawn has pointed out at one time or another, the interest of other advanced countries was divided between the urge to speed their own industrialization by drawing on the resources of Britain and the urge to protect themselves against British industrial supremacy. In the process of industrialization an advanced country would initially need Britain because (in the early stages at all events) it would benefit by drawing on the unique supply of the capital, machinery, and technical skills of Britain, and sometimes it had no alternative. Thus, it has been observed that time and again the first factories or machine workshops on the European continent were started by some Englishmen, the first native machines copied from some British design, the first railways were built by British contractors (with British locomotives, rails, technical staff, and capital). However, sooner or later its role could be displaced and these countries were then able to compete and even undersell Britain.

In the developing countries, on the other hand, the role of the foregin element has assumed a somewhat semipermanent or permanent status (in some cases even to an increasing degree). The dynamic enterprises (in agriculture, mining, power, and manufacturing) producing raw materials, semiprocessed or finished products, and to a certain degree in trade, banking and other services, have often been under foreign ownership and/or control, and may remain so for a long time to come. The question here is not whether foreign ownership and control is inherently undesirable, but rather whether it is so pervasive and in the area of strategic and crucial enterprises that the foreign domination makes the developing countries more exposed to external vulnerability and considerably lacking in their economic independence, and whether there is any prospect for its smooth orderly transition to national control at some future date. These enterprises often constitute a well-entrenched enclave, directly linked to the foreign economies and engaging in very little intercourse with the domestic sector (and, therefore, does not induce significant other domestic productive activities), but playing an important part in the economy for its major role in exports and imports as well as in being a substantial source of government revenues.

In the advanced countries industrialization has brought in its wake a greater degree of economic independence and a broadly based economic structure capable of self-generated and self-sustained growth. The irony for the developing countries is that the attempt at industrialization could instead lead to greater economic dependence especially if its import-content involves advanced stages of manufacturing with little possibility of import substitution. The growth of such industries would directly lead to greater foreign exchange requirements to ensure the steady flow of imported input requirements; these foreign exchanges must be obtained somehow lest the growth of such industries be thwarted.

The various aspects of the initial conditions referred to above are the matrix out of which there has emerged a pattern of colonial or semicolonial economic dependence which characterizes many contemporary developing countries. These initial conditions encompass a domestic and international constellation of factors which are not only economic in nature but also cover political, historical, social, and cultural factors as well. The pattern of colonial or semicolonial economic dependence is the product of the interplay of forces which have been at work for decades or even for centuries. It is, therefore, easier to succumb to its trend (and perhaps economically rational as well in the short run) than to pursue a deliberate policy and strategy which depart from it for the latter would have to cope with the deadweight of historical inheritance.

If the process of economic development is to be largely determined by autonomous private forces, the initial conditions must be more favorable than if the government takes on the major responsibility in guiding the process. It may well be that the greater the role of the government, the more formidable are the initial conditions that constitute obstacles to economic development. However, it may be

noted that in the developing countries, in general, governments could not exercise an all-embracing control over the
whole range of the production process: within this context, and compounded with the fact that many plans for
economic development are relying to a substantial degree
on foreign financing, the available options are limited and
the most that can be expected is an influence in some
facets of development. Even restricted facets of economic
development need a deliberate policy and strategy to
counter forces moving toward colonial and semicolonial
patterns of economic dependence. On the other hand,
policy and strategy are the product of political and social
forces that are strongly marked by the linkage between
decision making (and the power of carrying it out) and
economic strength. Without the confines of a framework
whereby there is a deliberate attempt at self-reliance and at
achieving a greater degree of economic independence, an
apparent economic progress is compatible with greater
economic dependence.

About two decades ago there were still lively debates
on the subject of planning for economic development.
Now it has been widely applied as a tool in the developing
countries which differ in their political systems as well as
in their stages of development although many plans have
not measured up to expectation in their actual performance. Some would argue that development planning
would not be effective unless there were radical political
and social transformations; some would attribute the
shortage in performance to an inadequate administrative
and organizational framework, and others to deficiencies
in methods and forms of planning. In any case, debates on
the advocacy and efficacy of planning imply that policy
and strategy for economic development do affect the
working of the mechanism for economic development. In
fact, it has become almost axiomatic to regard planning as
the means for promoting development, or even as the
panacea for economic development.

The theory underlying development planning seen

from its methodological or technical aspect is essentially the orthodox economic theory utilizing the norm of optimal allocation of resources applied to a certain notion with regard to what constitutes the mechanism for economic development. The use of macroeconomic plans as an instrument for formulating a development strategy has the advantage of permitting feasibility and consistency tests as well as ensuring optimal allocation of resources. Once the objectives have been defined, the following can proceed: *feasibility test* to ensure that the aggregate requirements of resources for achieving the plan objectives do not exceed aggregate available resources; *consistency test* to maintain equilibrium sectoral relationships and equalities of supply and demand for particular commodities; *optimality test* to ensure that there exists no other alternative method of resource allocation which can obtain the given objectives of the plan more efficiently. As such, the procedures involved are ethically and politically neutral and can be applied to any political and economic system regardless of the degree of government control and of the extent of the public ownership of the means of production. Too much obsession with the technical or methodological aspect of planning, however, could produce policy and strategy which ignore, or do not take into sufficient consideration, the basic initial conditions and their consequent effects.

In discussing or formulating a theory of economic development, one can assume the initial conditions or collapse them into some form of a notion of a universal state of underdevelopment; it cannot be said, however, that the working of the mechanism for economic development will not be affected by the divergent initial conditions nor that such divergence can justify the existence of the concept of a universal state of underdevelopment. Policy and strategy for economic development, therefore, cannot be based solely on some notion regarding the mechanism of economic development which ignores or oversimplifies the relevant initial conditions.

The process of economic development is a complex problem: while theories describing the mechanism for economic development can ignore, assume, or simplify the divergent initial conditions and differences in policies and strategies being adopted, these factors are an integral part of an economic development process. Its complexities arise because these factors and their intricate interrelationships often merit analyses and examination of their own insofar as the developing countries are concerned, rather than being assumed as given and taken for granted as predetermined variables. This proposition carries the implication that as long as the process cannot be regarded merely as the mechanism for economic development, the process of economic development covers areas beyond those that are strictly economic.

NOTES

1. The countries are, for example: Barbados, Bhutan, Botswana, Congo (People's Republic of), Equatorial Guinea, Fiji, Gabon, Gambia, Guyana, Kuwait, Lesotho, Mauritius, Swaziland, Western Samoa.
2. See *Handbook of International Trade and Development Statistics, Supplement 1970* (UN publication, Sales No. E/F.70.II.D.12), Table 6.11. The countries in this sample (where the figures in brackets indicate the percentage share of manufacturing in total GDP) are, on the one hand, Burundi (4), Chad (4), Dahomey (3), Gabon (4), Guinea (3), Lesotho (1), Liberia (4), Libya (2), Mauritania (1), and, on the other, Brazil (27), Chile (26), Egypt (23), Iran (32), Israel (23), Mexico (30), Singapore (52), Taiwan (21), Trinidad and Tobago (22), Uruguay (26).
3. See *World Economic Survey, 1969-1970* (UN publication, Sales No. E.71.II.C.1), Table A. 10. The countries in this sample (where the figures in brackets signify the percentage of adult literates) are, on the one hand, Chad (7), Ethiopia (5), Guinea (5), Mali (2), Mauritania (3), Niger (3), Senegal (6), Sierra Leone (7), Somalia (5), Togo (7), Upper Volta (7), and, on the other,

Argentina (91), Barbados (91), Chile (84), Costa Rica (84), Israel (84), Jamaica (82), Lebanon (86), Trinidad and Tobago (89), Uruguay (90).

4. Successful discovery and exploitation of natural resources can dramatically change the picture. In Libya, for example, within a six-year period (1962-68) gross domestic product at constant market prices has increased to more than fourfold. Although Libya's per capita GDP in 1958 was less than U.S. $120, in 1968 it was greater than that of the United Kingdom.

5. Adopted at the Ministerial Meeting of the Group of 77 on October 24, 1967. See *Proceedings of the United Nations Conference on Trade and Development, Second Session*, Vol. I, *Report and Annexes* (United Nations publication, Sales No. E.68.II.D.14), p. 440.

6. See the "Report of the Working Group of Fifteen of the Group of 77 on Special Measures to Be Taken in Favour of the Least Developed among the Developing Countries" (held at Geneva December 1-14, 1967) in *ibid.*, p. 453.

7. *Ibid.*, Resolution 24(II), p. 54.

8. See *Official Records of the Economic and Social Council, Fifty-first Session*, Supplement No. 7 (Document E/4990).

9. See *Review of International Trade and Development, 1970* (UN publication, Sales No. E.71.II.D.5), Table 1, p. 4.

10. If the non-Asian centrally planned economies are to be included as well, the distribution of the world's GNP in 1969 would be about 12.2 percent in the developing, 15.3 percent in the centrally planned, and 72.5 percent in the developed market economies.

11. R. B. Suhartono, "Material Poverty: The Plague of the Majority of Mankind," *World Justice*, June, 1969.

12. It has been suggested, for example, that the achievement of significant economies of scale requires a market of 10 to 15 million people. See E. A. G. Robinson (ed.), *Economic Consequences of the Size of Nations* (London: Macmillan, 1960). Also H. B. Chenery, "Patterns of Industrial Growth," *American Economic Review*, September, 1960.

13. See M. S. Wionczek (ed.), *Economic Co-operation in Latin America, Africa and Asia* (Cambridge: MIT, 1969).

14. See Havelock Brewster, *Industrial Integration Systems*, July 12, 1971, UNCTAD: Trade and Development Board (TD/B/345).

15. See M. S. Wionczek, "The Rise and the Decline of Latin

American Economic Integration," *Journal of Common Market Studies*, September, 1970.
16. See Kazushi Ohkawa and Henry Rosovsky, "The Role of Agriculture in Japanese Economic Development," in Carl Eicher and Lawrence Witt (eds.), *Agriculture in Economic Development* (New York: McGraw-Hill, 1964). See also Kenzo Kiga, "Characteristics of Japan's Economic Growth," *Studies on Developing Countries*, no. 32, Budapest 1968, which has placed a higher estimate, 68 percent, for the year 1880.
17. See D. Granick, *Soviet-Metal Fabricating and Economic Development: Practice versus Policy* (Madison: University of Wisconsin Press, 1967).
18. See E. L. Wheelwright and B. McFarlane, *The Chinese Road to Socialism* (New York: Monthly Review Press, 1970).
19. See H. Myint, An Inaugural Lecture, the London School of Economics and Political Science, *Economic Theory and Development Policy*, (London: Bell and Sons Ltd., 1967).
20. See J. R. Hicks, *Capital and Growth* (New York: Oxford University Press, 1965).
21. Myint, *Economic Theory and Development Policy*, p. 7.
22. Cf. S. Ishikawa, *Economic Development in Asian Perspective* (Tokyo: Kinokuniya, 1967).
23. Simon Kuznets, "Present Underdeveloped Countries and Past Growth Patterns," in Eastin Nelson (ed.), *Economic Growth* (Austin: University of Texas Press, 1960).
24. It has been suggested that "in almost all respects, except perhaps political weakness, Japan, before its industrialization, appeared to be similar to the populous underdeveloped countries of Asia" (*ibid.*, p. 24). See also C. K. Wilber, *The Soviet Model and Underdeveloped Countries* (Chapel Hill: University of North Carolina Press, 1969).
25. *Economic Development in Asian Perspective.*
26. Kuznets, "Present Underdeveloped Countries and Past Growth Patterns," p. 25.
27. *Ibid.*, pp. 23-24.
28. See E. J. Hobsbawm, *Industry and Empire* (Baltimore: Penguin Books, 1968).
29. See W. G. Hoffmann, *The Growth of Industrial Economies* (Manchester, Manchester University Press, 1958), pp. 24-41.
30. The effective rate of protection can be calculated from this formula:

$$p = \frac{\tau - \mu \, \tau \, M}{1 - M}$$

where τ is tariff on final goods, μ ratio of input to final goods tariffs, and M is import content.

31. See Morgens Boserup, "Agrarian Structure and Take-off," in W. W. Rostow (ed.), *The Economics of Take-off into Sustained Growth* (London: Macmillan, 1963). See also Paul Mantoux, *The Industrial Revolution in the Eighteenth Century* (New York: Harper and Row, 1961).

CHAPTER II

FACTORS AFFECTING ECONOMIC GROWTH

Although it has been increasingly recognized that economic development encroaches upon factors that are not strictly economic, the main problem of economic development is normally formulated in terms of how to transform a developing economy into one where a sustaining and continuing growth in its per capita income becomes a normal feature. Thus, for example, Chenery and Strout have formulated the idea that "the central problem of economic development is the transformation of a poor and stagnant economy into one whose normal condition is continuing growth."[1]

Such a formulation, whereby *growth* is identified as *development*, implicitly assumes that there exists a universal state of underdevelopment whose state will disappear as soon as the economy is capable of reaching sustained growth. Although, as may be recalled from the previous chapter, there are about 50 developing countries whose per capita GNP is lower than $200, the general characterization of a developing country as a poor economy is hard to visualize in view of the fact that there are more than 15 developing countries whose per capita GNP is higher than $500. Similarly, its stagnant aspect is difficult to conceptualize without specifically relating it to the time dimension and the particular rate of growth. Throughout 1955-65, there were more than 20 developing countries whose average annual rate of growth in gross domestic product was higher than 5 percent; though the average growth in Mexico during 1870-1950 was lower than 3 percent, in 1950-69 it was more than 6 percent. It may also be noted that for, say, Indonesia, a sustained and continuing growth in gross domestic product at an annual rate of 10 percent throughout a 35-year period will still not bring its per capita GDP to the present level in Israel (in 20 years it is still less than $50) within the conceptual construct described above. The central problem of economic development in Indonesia is already solved, although several decades afterwards its per capita GDP is still lower than those currently observed in contemporary developing countries.

In any event, the formulation of an economic development problem in such a manner is based on the consideration that whatever are the goals of any society, rising per capita incomes enlarge the options available for achieving these goals and are the means for their attainment. As it has been expressed by Millikan: "While self-sustaining growth will not in itself of necessity bring with it adequate progress toward all the other goals that countries seek . . . it can . . . be persuasively demonstrated that in the absence of per capita growth, significant progress towards most of these goals is impossible. Without growth, there can be no lasting alleviation of poverty, no industrialization, no important improvement in agriculture, no real amelioration of malnutrition, little progress in education or the spread of employment opportunities, and very low prospects of increased citizen participation."[2]

Formulating the problem of economic development in terms of the growth in per capita income considerably eases its exposition into manageable proportion: the problem can be broadly defined in terms of the identification of the growth determinants and the specification of the interrelationships among these determinants that will ensure steady growth. *Per capita income* is by definition the total aggregate income divided by the total number of population in a given country. Increased growth rate in per capita income, therefore, implies a larger difference between the growth rate in total income and the growth rate in population: provided that these two growth rates are independent, acceleration in the growth rate of per capita income can be achieved through decelerating the growth rate of population (advocates of population control in the developing countries, therefore, implicitly assume that such control does not adversely affect total income growth).

The remainder of this chapter will deal with the question of income growth. The subsequent chapter, on the other hand, will discuss problems relating to the interpretation of the meaning of per capita income.

Determinants of Growth

It follows from the preceding discussion that a theory describing the mechanism for economic development essentially deals with the question of what institutional, behavioral, technical, and equilibrating factors determine income and its rate of growth, and of how to facilitate the transformation of a developing economy into another characterized by the continuing growth in its per capita income. From the aggregative viewpoint, the income of a country (after allowing for some adjustments) is the total amount of production of goods and services which can be generated by its normal residents (nationals and nonnationals). It has long been postulated in the economic literature that the determinants of output or production are these productive inputs: *land* (natural resources or resource endowments), *labor*, and *capital*. In its broad and ultimate sense, the capability of an economy to generate the production of goods and services depends on the availability of the factors of production constituting the productive inputs and the manner by which these productive inputs are combined and transformed into output by men utilizing their technological, organizational, and managerial skills. Economists have generally agreed on the identification of income growth determinants, although not necessarily on the relationships that they thought existed among such determinants; these generally accepted growth determinants are natural resources, growth in labor force and skills, capital accumulation or investment, and technical progress.

Again it may be emphasized that the nineteenth-century world order is different from the twentieth-century one, which is unfavorable to the contemporary developing countries. In the nineteenth-century world order, one could characterize international trade as the "engine of growth" because of observable phenomena that economic growth was transmitted from the pioneers to some outer emerging countries in the rest of the world through resource discoveries and expansion in the arable land frontier by the opening up of virgin territories. The main commodities traded were textiles and other manufactures, on the one hand, and agriculture products and raw materials, on the other.[3]

Colonialism and the rapid expansion of transport and communication networks greatly aided resource-induced capital flows and economically useful migration. Migration from Western Europe to North America, for example, eased population pressure in the former during its transformation from agricultural into industrial societies, while at the same time it overcame the labor shortage in the latter. Expansion of the demand for agricultural and mineral products attracted investment and facilitated growth; some countries such as Burma and Thailand benefited from resource-induced growth in the neighboring countries by increasing rice production and exports, facilitated by a mere utilization of idle land. The constellation of the nineteenth-century world order was also favorable for the emergence of substantial manufacturing industries in some countries with high rates of growth which acted as the leading sectors.

Currently, the position of the contemporary developing countries within the international economic nexus could constitute more of a retarding factor to growth rather than a stimulus. The considerable difficulties confronting exporters of primary commodities have become familiar. Not all mineral products have bright prospects in the world market for the foreseeable future. Expansion of the arable land frontier is limited (and requires a formidable amount of resources) or nonexistent. The easing of population pressures on resources through emigration is out of the question.[4] The possibilities for investment and growth induced by further resource discoveries are probably more limited than they were during the nineteenth century. For these and other reasons, growth of per capita income in contemporary developing countries has been regarded as crucially dependent on the mobilization of resources which can bring rapid industrialization and increased agricultural productivity.

It can also be noted that so much of the productive inputs are now man-made that differences in the extent of resource endowments do not necessarily explain the variation in output levels nor their rates of growth.[5] In studies related to developed countries, natural resource endowments have not been found to be significant in explaining the variation in their output growth.[6] On the other hand, technical progress, the realized product of man's efforts in improving his knowledge, has been explicitly treated as a separate productive input.[7] Although there are difficulties in measurement, several economists (Auckrust, Bombach, Denison, Domar, Fabricant, Solow, Strumilin) have pointed out that in the many countries studied, an increase in the supply of capital and labor of unchanged quality does not explain more than half of the estimated growth of aggregate output; some two-thirds to more than nine-tenths of the increase in productivity are accounted for by technical progress.

Based on the United States data for 1909-57, Kuznets has observed, for example, that over 85 percent of the total growth of national income per person employed is attributable to the increased education of the labor force and the increased output per unit of input, due largely to economies of scale and the spread of technical knowledge.[8] The rapid increases of per capita incomes of the advanced countries cannot be explained solely by increases in the quantity of the conventional inputs; technology is the inner dynamics and the propulsive force for their growth, while at the same time it is the virtual monopoly of the industrialized countries.

Increasing attention has been given to the question of investment in "human capital" in the developing countries, recognizing the fact that growth does not depend solely on material inputs alone but more importantly on the availability of manpower needed for modern methods of production.[9] In the developing countries, rural and urban unemployment of unskilled labor often coexists with vacancies for skilled and semiskilled workers; on the other hand, there are also unemployed school graduates with specialized training. It is not clear whether the inadequate availability of skilled and semiskilled labor is partly responsible for underdevelopment (certainly the technological inferiority of the developing countries is due to the lack of applied knowledge), or whether such inadequacy is merely the symptom of underdevelopment.

In studies relating to the advanced countries, the contribution of technical progress or education on growth is merely that part of growth not specifically attributable to other specified inputs. Technical progress is embodied in capital: Kaldor and other economists have maintained that the introduction or infusion of knowledge into the growth process obtained mainly through the introduction of new equipment. The introduction of new equipment creates skill problems which can be learned; on the other hand, the provision of specialized skills without the necessary equipment does not necessarily produce increased output. On a more casual basis, one could observe in many developing countries downtrodden motor vehicles which are beyond repair in the advanced countries, and yet could still operate due to the ingenuity of local mechanics who often do not have formal training and education.

There is a substantial watershed between a developing and a developed economy and the transformation of the former into the latter involves a transitional process. In a sense there is a more or less broad consensus as to the principal changes that must occur during such a transformation, viz., improvement in human skills (managerial, organizational, technological), institutional changes and reform, increases in the rates of savings and investment, application of more productive methods of production, changes in the composition of domestic product, etc., although controversies arise regarding the sequential links comprising the transformation process. In the theory which approaches the problem of development in terms of the stages of growth, it has been maintained that there exists clearly defined and causally linked stages, somewhat containing an element of determinism.

In Rostow's concept of the "take-off into self-sustained growth," it has been argued that there is an identifiable watershed when growth becomes the normal trend: the transition can be usefully broken down into the period when the preconditions for growth are established, followed by a period of take-off in which there occurs an acceleration in the rate of growth triggered by the combination of critical changes in the economic, political, social, and institutional frameworks (a rise in the net investment from 5 to 10 percent or more of national income, the development of dynamic manufacturing industries setting the general pace of development, the emergence of political, social, and institutional frameworks favoring the leading sectors and transmitting their dynamics to other sectors, giving to growth an ongoing character).[10]

The concept relating to the set of critical changes has also been elaborated by other economists.[11] In connection with the take-off problem, Myint has suggested that "the central problem of [the developing] countries is not how to plan an immediate take-off, but how to compress the pre take-off phase into a few decades instead of a long period of a century or conceivably more which the Western countries are said to have taken."[12] Chenery and Strout, on the other hand, have argued that foreign assistance would make substantial differences possible in the transitional process, and have suggested that it is virtually a separate factor of production facilitating fuller use of domestic resources and temporarily relaxing the potential bottlenecks, implying, therefore, that it has a catalytic effect in enhancing savings and investment from domestic sources.[13] In the case of Israel and Taiwan, for example, it has been suggested that not only was growth accelerated through the provision of external capital, but the capability of each country to sustain further growth from its own resources was also significantly enhanced.[14]

Aggregative Framework

Economic growth is the product of the spontaneous action of the private forces (nationals and nonnationals) and the effect of government policy and strategy; in other words, there are autonomously determined and policy-induced growth factors. In an attempt to isolate the policy-induced factor, Maddison, using a sample of 22 countries and the data for 1950-65 (some of the countries in his sample do not belong to the present list of developing countries), has maintained that on the average about 2 of the annual growth rate of 5.6 percent can be attributed to the domestic policy effect of governments (the policy-induced growth rates range from less than 1 percent in Argentina, Chile, Pakistan, and Venezuela to greater than 3 percent in Spain, Taiwan, Thailand, and Yugoslavia): "all the policy-induced growth was due to increased factor inputs."[15]

Also in isolating the effect of economic policy on growth in South East Asia (Burma, Indonesia, Malaysia, and Thailand), Myint has argued that the orthodox type of economic policies (greater reliance on market forces, private enterprise, and outward-looking attitude toward foreign trade and enterprise) pursued by Malaysia, Philippines, and Thailand resulted in a more rapid economic growth during the post-war period than the newer and progressive development policies (Burma and Indonesia at one time leaned heavily on economic planning and large-scale intervention in economic life, combined with an inward-looking and even hostile attitude toward foreign trade and enterprise).[16] Whether one agrees or disagrees with these types of an assessment, government policy can be expected to affect the working of the mechanism for economic development; the efficacy of the policy, on the other hand, will be influenced by the stage of development already obtained.

In describing the mechanism for economic development (by identifying the growth in gross domestic product as an index of development performance), it is usually assumed that as a first approximation and *ceteris paribus*, and within a broad aggregative framework, the rate of growth of GDP in the developing countries is a function of the rate of investment.[17] The assumption underlying such a single-factor production function is that a change in investment will also be accompanied by a change in other cooperant factors such that the relation is maintained (in other words, changes in investment also represent changes in labor input which activates it as well as in all other inputs necessary for the transformation of investment into output).

For many economists, a high level of investment or capital accumulation has been regarded as the crucial element for growth; while some would question the validity of assigning so much weight on capital accumulation, and even if it were not the only significant variable, it remains nonetheless an important one. Although in an aggregative model it might be shown, theoretically as well as by applying econometric technique to available data, that investment can be regarded as the sole significant explanatory variable for the variation in GDP, the marginal contribution of other explanatory variables will become more and more statistically significant as one moves further in disaggregating the model.

If an economy is isolated and self-sufficient without foreign trade, the rate of growth of GDP is domestically determined and the rate of investment is defined by purely internal factors. Since in such a closed economy the rate of growth of GDP must be such that the rate of investment is equal to the rate of savings, equilibrium rate of growth can be maintained only if it is equal to the ratio of the rate of savings to the incremental capital output ratio.[18] However, an increase in the rate of investment can yield a corresponding growth in GDP only if there are available sufficient supplies of human skills: if such an increase in investment cannot be maintained without a decrease in its level of productivity below an acceptable minimum owing to the skill bottleneck, then growth is constrained by the skill limit. On the other hand, if skills availability is not a bottleneck, growth will be constrained by the savings limit.

In an open economy model, investment is determined by domestic savings as well as by external capital or foreign capital inflow. Allowing for the possibility of external assistance, equilibrium growth in an open economy can depart from the requirement of the balance between investment and domestic savings, as long as it satisfies the equilibrium condition that the corresponding level of income generates a difference between investment and domestic savings equal to the discrepancy between imports and exports financed by such external assistance.

Defining *savings-investment gap* as the difference between the domestic savings which the economy is capable of generating and the gross investment required to attain a given rate of growth of GDP, and *export-import gap* as the difference between the level of export earnings which the economy is able to supply and the required imports corresponding to the given rate of growth, equilibrium growth is maintained only if simultaneously the savings-investment gap is equal to the export-import gap, which in turn is equal to available foreign capital flow. Depending on the nature of the structural equations, Chenery and Strout have suggested the existence of the savings and trade limits to growth and it has been argued further that "despite the possibilities of variation, however, there is a considerable likelihood that if growth is accelerated from a low income level the phases will succeed each other in the order of . . . (I) Skill-limited Growth; (II) Savings-limited Growth; (III) Trade-limited Growth."[19]

Thus, the basic notion underlying what has commonly been known as the "two-gap analysis" is that there are at least two independent resources constraints on the growth of the developing countries, viz., the savings-constraint (availability of savings for investment) and the trade-constraint (availability of foreign exchange for importing specific commodities for current production and investment).[20] On the other hand, Weisskopf, using a sample of 44 countries, has concluded that there appears to be good reason to question the significance commonly attributed to the trade constraint as an independent limit on growth. His results based on this sample suggest that a limiting trade-constraint on growth has been a relatively infrequent phenomenon in the postwar experience of the developing countries.[21]

What has emerged from the preceding discussion on the aggregative model is that growth in the developing countries involves two scarce factors: domestic savings and foreign capital inflow. Crucial to the growth-inducing effect on foreign capital inflow is the basic implicit assumption that the relationship between it and domestic savings is one of complementarity rather than that of substitutability. In practice, however, such relationship does not necessarily maintain, as some studies cited in the subsequent discussion appear to suggest.

Domestic Savings

In terms of the population distribution in 1965, about three-fourths of the population in the developing countries were from those where the average ratios of savings to GDP for the years 1963-65 were below the average of 15 percent. For the years 1966-68, the average rate of savings for the developing countries was 16.1 percent (in the developed market economies, it was 22.4 percent); the distribution of the savings rates was as follows:

PERCENTAGE DISTRIBUTION OF GROSS DOMESTIC SAVINGS RATES[a]
IN THE DEVELOPING COUNTRIES, 1966-68 AVERAGES

Savings rates in percent	Number of developing countries
Under 5.0	10
5.1-10.0	14
10.1-15.0	25
15.1-20.0	14
20.1-25.0	10
Over 25.0	9

Source: World Economic Survey, 1969-1970, pp. 208-10.
[a]Defined as ratios of gross domestic savings to gross domestic product measured at 1960 market prices.

It may be noted that out of the 51 countries with below-average savings rates, 25 (Africa 3, Asia 7, Western Hemisphere 15) had higher-than-average per capita GDP. On the other hand, out of the 30 countries with higher-than-average savings rates, 8 (in Africa 5, Asia 3) were from those with below-average per capita GDP.

Following the view held by Keynes in his general theory, it has been normally assumed that savings is directly related to income. As applied to the developing countries, the hypothesis of the vicious circle of poverty states that income is low because investment is low, investment is low because savings is low, savings is low because income is low, etc.[22] This hypothesis can be put in juxtaposition with these illustrative figures for the saving rates (as defined above) in selected countries (where figures in brackets indicate per capita income in U.S. dollars for 1967): Uganda 23.9 (82); Gabon 43.7 (427); Chile 9.4 (473); and Israel 4.6 (1167).

It might be too simplistic to postulate that savings is a straightforward function of income, for the developed as well as the developing countries. First, using evidence for the United States only, Duesenberry[23] has suggested that "according to our hypothesis, the savings rate is independent of the absolute level of income" because of the so-called demonstration-effect. As the hypothesis is applied to the developing countries, Nurkse[24] has remarked that given the very great discrepancies in the levels of living, the contact of poorer with richer nations may affect the demand for social legislation and industrial labor standards as well as the demand for modern luxuries, may stimulate desires before it improves productivity, may impel countries to keep outlays above what is warranted by the capacity to produce, so that the presence or the mere knowledge of new goods and new methods of consumption tends to lower the propensity to save.

Secondly, Houthakker and Friend-Taubman studies have demonstrated that almost the entire variation in personal savings is explained by the variation in nonlabor income.[25] Third, as presumed by Haavelmo, domestic savings could be negative if foreign capital inflow is very large; in studies related to some developing countries, it has been suggested that foreign capital inflow tends to reduce domestic savings.[26] (In other words, the relationship between the two is one of substitutability rather than that of complementarity.)

It can be noted that aggregate savings consist of personal and public savings, the latter being determined by government current expenditures and revenues. Revenues from direct taxation are on the average probably not more than 5 percent of national income in the developing countries, in contrast to almost 20 percent in the developed economies. Lower average income might be a disadvantage to the potential for direct taxation; on the other hand, as may be recalled from the previous chapter, there might be greater inequality in the distribution of income in some developing countries which could offset such disadvantage. Lewis has suggested that although many developing countries tax high personal incomes at the same rate as such incomes are taxed in the developed economies, "the number of persons liable to pay income tax is very much smaller, typically less than 3 percent of the occupied population compared with 50 percent in the developed economies."[27] Kaldor has described in detail the political constraints for raising taxes in a number of countries.[28] Little, on the other hand, has argued that wealthy individuals whose income is largely derived from the land escape much more lightly than those whose income is derived from other sources.[29]

From the expenditure side, the position of the contemporary developing countries is not very favorable. In the developed countries, laws, institutions, and expenditures relating to social welfare were preceded by the improvement in general economic conditions resulting from economic growth; in some, acceleration of capital accumulation occurred regardless of its impact on the social welfare of the general populace. By contrast, mobilization of domestic resources in contemporary developing countries must take place within the context of the need for expenditures on social services (social welfare, health, education) having been taken for granted, minimum wage and trade union laws having been adopted, etc.

Many developing countries are overurbanized in the sense that larger proportions of their population are in urban areas than are warranted by their levels of development (a much smaller percentage of the labor force is engaged in nonagricultural occupation than was the case in the industrialized countries at their comparable levels of urbanization, where urbanization is both an antecedent and a consequence of rapid industrialization).[30] In the developing countries, the rapid rate of urbanization has not usually been the concomitant of economic growth; rather, it reflects other influences, "particularly lack of progress in the agricultural sector and the mounting pressure on rural workers—especially the young peasants and those with little prospect of acquiring land—of underemployment and deteriorating levels of living."[31] Whether it is due to the pull factor from the cities, or the push factor from the limited opportunities in the rural areas, the flow from rural to urban centers has exceeded the capability to create urban employment. Thus, there has been a phenomenon of increasing urban unemployment expanding the demand for urban services but generating neither increased output nor higher tax revenues to finance such services.[32]

Tensions have made some developing countries perceive the necessity for devoting larger shares of their resources for military and defense purposes than in most developed countries. Military outlays in the developing countries probably run to more than $20 billion annually, greater than the amount of aid received and about 7 percent of their combined GNP, have high import-content and foreign exchange requirements, and do not directly generate greater growth of output in the domestic sector. It has been remarked that "on the average, undernourished Asian peoples spend 5.9 percent of their national income for defense purposes, a figure that rises to 11.6 percent for the Arab States."[33]

Investment

For the years 1966-68, the average of the rates of gross domestic investment in the developing countries was 17.4 percent (in the developed market economies the corresponding figure was 24.0 percent). The percentage distribution of these rates is as follows:

64   *Development—Lessons for the Future*

PERCENTAGE DISTRIBUTION OF GROSS DOMESTIC INVESTMENT RATES[a] IN THE DEVELOPING COUNTRIES, 1966-68 AVERAGES

Investment rates in percent	Number of developing countries
5.1-10.0	3
10.1-15.0	25
15.1-20.0	35
20.1-25.0	14
Over 25.0	5

Source: World Economic Survey, 1969-1970, pp. 208-10.
[a]Ratios of gross domestic fixed capital formation, or, in some countries, gross domestic capital formation, to gross domestic product measured at constant 1960 market prices.

It may be noted that comparability of the figures for the investment rate is difficult to ascertain because of the variation in the relative prices of capital goods.[34]

In a very broad and approximate sense, however, and by applying the rule of thumb that around 2 to 4 percent of GDP is for depreciation, it appears that the critical effort involved insofar as the rate of net investment is concerned (10 percent or more) has been attained in at least more than 50 developing countries. On the other hand, it will be too rash to conclude therefrom that in these countries per capita income has reached a self-sustaining growth. It is quite conceivable that the past take-off into self-sustaining growth as observed in the advanced countries is attributable to the unleashing of the gathering forces of growth which manifested themselves in a sudden burst of the investment rate, which in turn acted as the catalyst of growth. In this instance, the sudden increase in investment rate is not the cause of self-sustaining growth, but rather it is the mere symptom of the latent forces of growth. Similarly, an observed low rate of investment is not necessarily the cause of underdevelopment, but might instead be the mere symptom of it and the causes must be sought elsewhere. In this instance, the sudden increase in investment rate does not guarantee self-sustaining growth without the concomitant removal of the basic causes of underdevelopment.

In a macroaggregate economic planning, two coefficients relating to the concept of capital have been widely utilized, viz., capital coefficient or capital-output ratio, and incremental capital-output ratio or the amount of investment needed to produce a given increase in output. It should be emphasized, however, that these relations are merely statistical and do not necessarily indicate causal relationship. The coefficients can change according to different levels of development or because of other reasons.

Bicanic has observed that in a stagnating or slowly growing economy, where labor is relatively abundant and capital scarce, the coefficient tends to be low (2:1); during the initial stage of development it tends to rise (to 6:1 or more); subsequently, it tends to decrease.[35] It has been argued further that historically there have occurred three distinguishable thresholds which coincide with different industrial revolutions: the first took place toward the end of the eighteenth and up to the middle of the nineteenth centuries, based on coal, steam, steel, and railways; the second began to take place in the seventies of the nineteenth century, based on the combustion engine, oil, and electricity; the third in mid-twentieth century, based on automation, electronics, nuclear energy, and the chemical industry. In each initial stage of these industrial revolutions, there was an upward movement of the capital coefficient. The difficulty faced by the developing countries in overcoming their technological inferiority is that these three industrial revolutions must all be compressed over one time period, affecting the nature of the capital coefficient.

In the developing countries, there is an observed wide range in the values of the estimated incremental capital output ratio, which are found to differ by a multiple of

ten; based on the data for 1960-67, the estimated value for
the high-growth group of developing countries was 2.5, for
the medium-growth 3.1, and for the low-growth 6.2.[36]
Without detailed country studies it is not possible to
determine whether differences in the growth rates are
attributable to differences in the values of the capital
coefficient (which could partly reflect the productivity of
investment being undertaken), or whether the differences
in the values are due to the differences in the stage of
development which affect the investment requirement. It
may be recalled from the previous chapter, however, that
high growth has occurred mostly in the richer (and more
industrialized) developing countries, while low growth has
generally occurred in the poorer (and less industrialized)
economies. If income is the main determinant of savings,
and savings the main determinant of investment, then the
greater difficulties of the poorer developing countries to
generate higher investment rates are further handicapped
by the high value of incremental capital-output ratio
(conversely, the relative ease in generating greater investment rates in the richer countries is benefited further by
the lower value of the incremental capital-output ratio).

Capital coefficient and incremental capital-output ratio
are variables subject to modification and are greatly
affected by the strategy and policy of economic development being pursued, as well as differences in the initial
conditions of the countries. Different production sectors
have different sectoral capital-output ratios. The ratios are
high in infrastructure and energy (rails, road, water, air
transport and communication, electricity); in mining; in
agriculture relating to irrigation, forest clearance, land
reclamation; etc. They are low in light industries such as
textiles and wearing apparel; food processing; beverage and
tobacco; leather; etc. In addition to the sectoral makeup of
production and its consequent capital mix, the ratios are
also affected by the nature and durability of goods being
produced; by technical progress; and by measures adopted
to improve the efficiency in the use of existing capital.

Foreign Capital Inflow

Domestic investment can be financed through domestic savings and foreign capital inflows. Technically, and disregarding the possible direct and indirect adverse effects of foreign capital inflows, its increase, which facilitates an increase in domestic investment, can accelerate the growth in income. In practice, even the purely narrow aspect relating to the growth-inducing effect of foreign capital inflows is a controversial subject.

Apart from the impact of the Marshall Plan on the economies of Western Europe, examples for the substantial growth-effect of foreign capital inflows have normally been referred to Greece, Israel, South Korea, and Taiwan. The initial conditions of these economies are by no means typical of the developing countries; besides, in these four countries (where Greece is not even listed as a developing economy), the sixteen years' average figures for the annual ratios of foreign capital inflows to their respective GDP and nonresidential investment are relatively high:

EXTERNAL FINANCE, 1950-65

Country	Average of annual ratios, in percent		Net receipts per capita, annual average in U.S. dollars, 1960-65		Per capita BNP, 1965 in U.S. dollars
	of GDP	of non-residential investment	Private capital	Official aid	
Greece	7.6	68.5	32.2	5.5	600
Israel	19.1	100.0	166.2	46.2	1130
South Korea	8.3*	94.3*	2.7	7.7	120
Taiwan	5.4	44.3	2.3	6.3	200

Sources: Maddison, Economic Progress and Policies in Developing Countries; World Bank Atlas, 1967 ed.

*1953-65.

By way of comparison, it can be noted that the average of
the ratios of net foreign capital inflows to the whole
developing countries is less than 4 percent of their combined GDP; in 54 developing countries (including Israel,
South Korea, and Taiwan), the average net receipts per
capita throughout 1961-65 was $4.39 ($3.29 official,
$1.10 private).[37]

In 1969, UNCTAD figures indicate that the net flows
of financial resources (disbursements) to the developing
countries amounted to about $12.8 billion; the major
components are bilateral official flows from the developed
market economies $6.0 billions, private flows $5.4 billions
($2.5 billions of which are in the form of direct invest-
ment), and multilateral agencies $1.1 billions. On the other
hand, capital outflows from the developing countries
amounted to $12.1 billions, $7.0 of which are for interest
and investment income payments (net). It has been
remarked that over the period 1960-69, there was

> a persistent tendency for the proportion of the develop-
> ing countries' foreign exchange resources devoted to
> imports to decline as the proportion devoted to the
> outflow of profits, interest and indigenous capital has
> increased. Put in a different way, these outflows have
> increased at a much faster rate during this period than
> the total inflow of resources. For *all* developing coun-
> tries, interest and investment income payments
> amounted to $7 billion in 1969, about 70 percent of
> which consisted of profits and dividends. Statistics of
> amortization payments . . . indicate that repayments of
> external debt increased at an average annual rate of 11
> percent during the period 1963-1967, reaching almost
> $2.5 billion per year by 1967.[38]

It can also be noted that throughout 1960-67, the rates of
growth of official and private flows (from the developed
market economies) were 6.7 and 4.1 percent, respectively,
(direct investment at a mere 1.9 percent); throughout

1963-67, the average annual rate of growth of payments on account of gross investment income was 12 percent, where interest payments grew faster than the payments for dividends and profits.

The statistics cited above seem to indicate that in global terms, foreign capital inflows to the developing countries (in conjunction with the required outflow) could not be expected to become a major determinant of accelerated growth, although the inflows might be crucial in preventing stagnation or deceleration to take place. In some developing countries foreign capital inflows are large and significant enough to facilitate growth to occur without its consequent strain on the balance of payments; the forces of growth might have been there and foreign capital inflows might have permitted better achievement than otherwise would be the case.

In some, however, foreign capital inflows could be in the form of stop-gap measures to ease the balance of payments pressures, where the pressures are not necessarily related to growth but rather arise from amortization and interest payments of past accumulated debt which has reached a critical level (whether or not such debt accumulation has directly contributed to growth, e.g., for armaments); from remittances of profits and dividends of past private foreign investment (especially in those industries which do not generate exports or whose import saving effect is not significant); from the high cost of industrialization (establishing industries with high import-content in the face of stagnant or declining export revenues); from indigenous and foreign private capital outflows; etc. Some economies might be sinking deeper and deeper into the forces of stagnation and foreign capital inflows might merely be a device to prevent bankruptcy. Needless to say, these examples of foreign capital inflows are fundamentally different from each other and thus it is hazardous to generalize on the growth-effect of foreign capital inflows without further examining the nature of these inflows.

Aid

A major component of foreign capital inflows to the developing countries is bilateral and multilateral aid. Although in practice aid can be deflected and rather than becoming a complement can become a substitute for domestic resources instead, *ceteris paribus* any aid which increases investment will accelerate growth. Thus, the effectiveness of aid is usually measured in terms of its effect on growth, which could also be expected subsequently to become self-sustaining. Chenery and Strout have argued that their examples

> support the theoretical conclusion that the achievement of a high rate of growth, even if it has to be initially supported by large amounts of external capital, is likely to be the most important element in the long-term effectiveness of assistance. The substantial increases in internal savings ratios that have been achieved in a decade of strong growth . . . demonstrate the rapidity with which aid-sustained growth can be transformed into self-sustained growth once rapid development has taken hold.[39]

Griffin and Enos, on the other hand, have suggested that if anything, "aid may have retarded development by leading to lower domestic savings, by distorting the composition of investment and thereby raising the capital-output ratio, by frustrating the emergence of an indigenous entrepreneurial class, and by inhibiting institutional reforms."[40] Instead of obtaining evidence for growth induced by aid, they have observed

> the opposite hypothesis is closer to the truth: in general, foreign assistance is not associated with progress and, indeed, may deter it. If the growth which a nation achieves, or fails to achieve, is related to the assistance it receives, one finds that there is no support for the view

that aid encourages growth. . . . Taking the average rate of growth of GNP over the years 1957-64 for the twelve (developing Western Hemisphere) countries for which figures are available, we find that it is inversely related to the ratio of foreign aid to GNP.[41]

Without disputing the possibilities for its growth-inducing effect, or its retarding and distorting consequences, it might be questioned whether relating growth to aid as a standard measure for aid effectiveness is particularly relevant (especially if the period of observation is relatively short), given the considerable diversity existing within the developing countries. It will take considerable resources (and time span) for Tanzania, for example, to attain the infrastructural development which in Taiwan has already been taken for granted: aid to the former utilized for the development of infrastructure, which within a decade after its disbursement might not appreciably increase the growth rate need not be less effective compared to the same amount of aid disbursed to the latter which could immediately be seen to accelerate growth. Nor could it be said that the initially high capital coefficient for Tanzania is necessarily a distortion in its composition of investment seen from the long-term perspective. Generalization based on the simple growth performance in the face of complex diversity in the initial conditions is apt to be fallacious.

To discuss aid within the context of growth assumes that its disbursement is based purely on economic consideration, and could lead to the proposition that it should be concentrated on the richer and more industrialized developing countries (these are more likely to demonstrate accelerated, and subsequently self-sustaining, growth), further enhancing the tendency for growth polarization. It has been observed that "the pattern of financial aid flows during the 1960s did not reflect any global development strategy on the part of donors, which would have eased the foreign exchange constraints of the slower-growing devel-

oping countries."[42] Access to aid differs from one country
to another, but aid tends to be concentrated on the richer
countries whose population constitute the minority, and
dispersed over the majority residing in the poorer countries.

Bhagwati has noted that in 1964 (and other earlier
years as well), from a total number of 105 developing
countries, 96 percent of their population received less than
$10 per capita net aid, whereas the remaining 4 percent,
residing in the favored areas, managed to get more.[43] His
figures also indicate that throughout 1960-63, more than
two-thirds of the population in the developing countries
received less than $2 per capita net aid. Furthermore, the
distribution of aid does not appear to favor the poorer
developing countries:

**DEVELOPING COUNTRIES: BILATERAL NET AID
RECEIPTS (1964) AND GROSS DOMESTIC PRODUCT
(1965), U.S. DOLLARS PER CAPITA**

	Number of countries with GDP				
Aid receipts	Under 100	100 to under 200	200 to under 500	500 and over	Total
Under 2.0	13	4	11	8	36
2.0-9.9	17	9	19	4	49
10.0-19.9	1	5	2	3	11
20.0-49.9	1	1	4	1	7
50.0 and over	0	0	1	1	2

Source: J. N. Bhagwati, Amount and Sharing of Aid (Washington: Overseas
Development Council, 1970), p. 67.

While the rhetoric of aid as the miracle tool for
smashing the tripod of poverty, disease, and ignorance has
often been aired, its consequent exhiliarating exuberance
has been followed by the ebb permeating from the growing
pessimism and disillusion. Rhetoric, however, is a cobweb
strangling the victim by its eloquence. It creates a state of

mind whereby a simple solution could be offered to a simplistic notion of the development problem and thus aid needs to be justified by its dramatic impact. Development is a complex problem requiring a long and arduous process which can defy dramatization, the more so in countries that are at the lowest stage of development, still groping frustratingly with the overwhelming problem of constructing from scratch the conditions that are already existing in the more developed developing countries. Dramatic demonstration for its effectiveness formulated in terms of accelerated and self-sustaining growth requires that it should be allocated only to countries with the best prospect for growth given a certain amount of aid; these countries are more likely to be a selected group among those of the more developed developing countries.

In any event, the past aid allocation does not seem to be primarily determined by economic consideration. In examining the pattern of aid allocation, Piatier has come to the conclusion that aid is not adjusted to the population size of the recipients; it is by no means adjusted to the situation of the beneficiaries; its effectiveness seems to bear no relation to the efforts made; and "the political factor explains certain concentrations of resources: nothing, or as little as possible to the countries politically, emotionally or ideologically at odds with the donor (Guinea, in the French-speaking group); often, too, nothing, or as little as possible, to poor but politically reliable countries: resources are withheld to maneuver elsewhere."[44] It has been remarked further that "the maximum is earmarked for actual or potential allies whose political situation is unstable and where it is hoped that a little economic wellbeing will restore internal equilibrium and confirm loyalty." As it has been observed by Griffin and Enos, "foreign aid tends to strengthen the status quo; it enables those in power to evade and avoid fundamental reforms; it does little more than patch plaster on the deteriorating social edifice."[45] To expect an economic miracle from economically unrelated aid could easily lead to illusion.

In recent years, aid has been scrutinized, for example, in studies commonly known as the Jackson Report, the Pearson Report, etc. The subject of aid has been obfuscated by the confusion regarding its objectives, but in any case there has been disillusion in the donor countries. In the case of the United States, Willard Thorp has observed that

> Since 1965, the proposals for foreign aid put forward by the President have met with more and more difficulty . . . there was considerable talk about rat-holes, dictatorships, corruption, balance of payments, the threats of communism, the brotherhood of man, India and the responsibilities of global leadership. . . . And pent-up dismay over the Vietnam situation found an outlet in attacking foreign aid.[46]

As described by Thorp, aid has been viewed by the U.S. Congress to be "obsolete, outmoded and unrealistic, mindless, a boondoggle, a giveaway by Uncle Santa Claus, and a bureaucratic maze beyond comprehension, consisting of waste, frauds, sham, friends lost, enemies made and hopes dashed." The critics of aid, on the other hand, have argued that aid is an instrument for "domesticating" the developing countries (Denis Goulet); that it is seriously ill-conceived, but contains the "strategy for maximizing U.S. self-interest," which has been considered as "increasingly narrow and para-military" in nature (Michael Hudson); that the multilateral agencies have exercised "leverage," i.e., "the use of aid to influence the policies of developing countries in one way or another" (Teresa Hayter).[47] Some developing countries have told donors to take their aid and "go to hell."

It does not appear, however, that the question of what motivates aid is of particular importance to the developing countries. Despite the rhetoric, it will be naive to expect

that the advanced countries are fulfilling the messianic role
for global development through aid. It is not a charity and
even if it is intended to be, it is undesirable and definitely
inadequate to meet the global challenge of development. It
creates a state of mind-mitigating self-reliance. Aid as
charity is a relation between superiority and inferiority, a
human indignity. Of little value is a few dollars' aid that
requires one to tolerate the paternalistic and overbearing
attitude of the plutocrat, one who, adopting Galbraith's
prose, "came to the aid of the poor only after a careful
consideration of their worth, his ability to spare from his
needs and the realistic likelihood of revolt and disorder if
he abstained . . . who believed withal that God inspired his
enterprise and generosity and often said so."[48] Self-
righteous in dictating what is good and bad for the poor
even in areas remotely far from the ordinary experience of
the plutocrat—this type of relation is inherent in charity
and is not what the developing countries seek.

The deadweight of history pulls the developing countries in the state of underdevelopment, the forces of
technological progress and obsolescence push them in a
state of perpetual underdevelopment. These formidable
factors constitute staggering obstacles which can overcome
a pessimist, make one resign and meekly follow the trend
of history; on the other hand, the overwhelming obstacles
can be considered a challenge to be overcome through
vigorous and resolute efforts. It is precisely because there
exist powerful and formidable forces obstructing development that a resolute objective for the strategy and policy
of economic development is an absolute essential. The
relevance of economic theories evolving in advanced and
industrialized economies to the contemporary developing
countries has increasingly been questioned; Myrdal, for
one, has testified to the bankruptcy of the conventional
wisdom.[49] Only the developing countries can light the
spark, rather than dictate the initiative of the rich.

Aid that is not a charity can be quite costly: its waste
cannot be recovered, but nevertheless its consequent costs

have to be borne. Accordingly, regardless of its underlying motive, aid has to be scrutinized by the recipient from the totality of its own national self-interest and self-esteem. Aid should be sought and received only if it enhances national economic development, which lessens economic dependence, where growth is merely but one aspect, a necessary but not sufficient condition. While the possible considerable benefits of aid should not be underestimated, it is a mere makeshift palliative, and can become addictive. Even when aid accelerates growth, it should be noted that higher income means greater demand for goods and services, which unless it can be matched by the increased production resulting from growth, would imply higher import requirements. These higher imports, in conjunction with interests and repayments, could lead to greater future external dependence, rather than contribute to the achievement of greater economic independence. Without a strategy of self-reliance, the need for aid could become cumulative: *aid generates the need for more aid*. Without an objective of attaining greater economic independence, a country can sink deeper and deeper into the position of external vulnerability and dependence. Aid should, therefore, be examined by the recipient within the context of the long-term strategy for economic development, geared to self-reliance and the attainment of economic independence: aid should be subordinated to this strategy, rather than the strategy being defined within the confine of projected aid to be forthcoming.

Private Flows

In the case of foreign private investment, there is a clear-cut profit motive on the part of the investors. There have been many studies devoted to the relation between exploitation and foreign investment, considered to be inherent and inevitable in the quest of profit motive, raising the specter of imperialism, incursion, and foreign domination, etc. On the other hand, many developing countries are competing among themselves in attracting foreign private investment, through offers of favorable climate and incentives such as tax holidays, accelerated depreciation allowance, special facilities and promotional privileges, etc., incentives which are not necessarily offered to domestic indigenous enterprises and could even be harmful to their emergence or survival. Apparently some types of foreign private investment are undesirable, especially those with a colonial or semicolonial setup and flavor; on the other hand, it has been recognized that foreign investment is essential in order to compensate for inadequate domestic financial resources and skills, to facilitate access to modern technology and foreign marketing network, etc. Mexico was one of the countries vehemently opposed to foreign private investment in prewar years, but it has modified its position since 1945. The Soviet Union is seeking private foreign capital to develop its vast natural resources in Siberia.

During the nineteenth-century world order, the United Kingdom was the dominant source for foreign private capital flows from the center to the periphery of the world economy, followed by France and Germany; at one time, the ratio of foreign investment to GNP in UK reached as high as 7 percent.[50] The capital flows were of the resource-induced type of investment, to colonies or independent countries such as Argentina, Brazil, Chile, Mexico, enhanced by the rapid improvement in transport and communication network. An overwhelming part (about three-fourths) of the capital flows was in bond issues or portfolio investment, while in the colonies the foreign investment originated mostly from the metropolitan powers: colonial power and military strength were sufficient to guarantee the investment against default.[51] It may be noted that while on a global-scale capital flows were characterized by the preponderance of portfolio investment, more than two-thirds of the latter were accounted for by Europe and the countries of European settlement, while the larger share of the direct or equity investment went to Asia, Africa, and the Western Hemisphere.[52] In the colonies, direct investment occurred in plantation and mining, while the portfolio investment was used mainly to finance the supporting infrastructure.

Regardless of its growth-effect, the rapid influx of foreign investment in the nineteenth-century world order apparently did not result in the development of the periphery. There are many countries in the periphery who were supposedly to benefit from the growth effect of such nature (in any case they have attained relatively high per capita incomes due to their rich natural resources), but they still belong to the list of the contemporary developing countries. In fact, it may well be that the structure of underdevelopment was established and consolidated thereby, so that the period saw the growth of underdevelopment in the periphery. Singer has argued that the concentration on exports of food and raw materials to the industrialized countries, largely as the result of investment by the latter, has been unfortunate for the developing countries for two reasons: first, because it removed most of the secondary and cumulative effects of investment from the country in which the investment took place to the investing country; and secondly, because it diverted the developing countries into those types of activities offering less scope for technical progress, and withheld from the course of their economic history a central factor of dynamic radiation which has revolutionized society in the industrialized countries.[53] Growth that occurred in the periphery was diffused from the center rather than the product of its own internal dynamics.

In the colonies and independent countries alike, the growth of the enclaves' economy with direct linkages to the metropolitan countries but insulated from the domestic economy created sectoral dislocations and disparities in productivity, weak inter- and intrasectoral relationships within the domestic economy, associated with the structures of external dependence and vulnerability, with little or no contribution to the development of indigenous technical, organizational, and managerial skills. In some there were alliances between large foreign enterprises and immigrant or native inhabitants serving the metropolitan interest. The nature of economic control resulting from private investment made the colonies appear as a subsidiary company, with the native inhabitants as dispensable blue collar workers, immigrants as white collars, foreigners as the executive, and the colonial government as policemen securing law and order and guarding the sanctity of private property.[54]

Subsequently the center of international finance shifted more and more toward New York. Today guarantees against default and the credit worthiness of the developing countries might be insufficient to warrant the raising of funds through bond issues on a substantial scale except for a few countries (Israel is a special case because the purchasers of its bonds are mostly the Jewish communities overseas). It has been observed that "there continues to be a striking contrast between the era preceding the Great Depression, characterized by intense portfolio investment, and the period since the Second World War, during which direct investment has become by far the largest component of capital flows to developing countries."[55]

Loan capital is still an important component of the private capital flows, but its nature is different from the earlier type or portfolio investment (government or private enterprise which obtained the portfolio investment through the international money market could utilize it according to their own needs and objectives). A substantial part of the loan capital consists of guaranteed private export credits (in 1969 constituting about one-third of private capital flows, while the rest was closely associated with the exigencies of private direct investment). UNCTAD has noted that

Since 1960, the most impressive gains in private flows have been recorded by guaranteed export credits, which

had more than quadrupled by 1969; most of these gains
are accounted for by credits exceeding five years dura-
tion; nevertheless, that the terms for commercial credit
are relatively hard is shown by the fact that 41 percent
of total debt service payments of developing countries
in 1968 was on account of such credits, although they
represented only 20 percent of total outstanding debt.[56]

Probably more important than the state of private
investors' confidence in determining the trend for the
preponderance of direct rather than portfolio investment
in the contemporary international capital market is the
recent phenomenal growth of the so-called multinational
corporations facilitated through technological and organizational innovation. These are the giant or large corporations with a global organizational network, acquired
through the parent companies having opened up branches
and subsidiaries, or having engaged in joint ventures, in
foreign countries.[57] A multinational corporation accordingly possesses enormous technological, organizational,
and managerial talents, vast financial resources, and
through its worldwide organizational network, has considerable flexibility in its efforts toward global profit
maximization.

Sydney Rolfe has estimated that the global total book
value of direct private investment (accumulated assets) in
1966 was about $89.5 billion, about 61 percent of which
was accounted for by United States capital, 18 percent by
the United Kingdom, and slightly less than 9 percent by
the combined capital of Canada, France, and Germany.[58]
About one-third of this total was in the developing
countries; since the figures are compiled from OECD-DAC
data, there is an overestimation due to the inclusion of
certain southern European countries.

The average annual rate of return from direct private
investment in the developing countries is perhaps about 15
percent or more (considerably higher in petroleum-produc-
ing countries), where the lower limit is likely to be

underestimated, partly because of transactions between the parent companies and their foreign affiliates, in effect an internal transaction within a multinational corporation which is subject to price manipulation. On the other hand, the average annual rates of return in the developed countries are probably in the range of 7 to 10 percent. If these figures are correct, the rate of return in the developing countries is higher than the rate of return in the developed economies. Since far more direct private investment has occurred in the latter, it appears that the rate of return is not the primary determinant of the investment flow.

Although less than one-third of U.S. direct investment flows to the developing countries, its sheer magnitude puts it into a significant position: in 1966, more than 55 percent of the book value of direct investment in the developing countries were accounted for by U.S. capital. In 1970, according to the *Survey of Current Business*, nearly two-fifths of U.S. direct investment in the developing countries was in petroleum (more than half if other mining and smelting, concentrated mostly in copper and aluminum industries, were to be included), and slightly over one-fourth in manufacturing. It can be noted that nearly 70 percent of U.S. direct investment in the developing countries was in the Western Hemisphere, nearly one-third of which was in the manufacturing sector: such investment in manufacturing alone already constitutes nearly 70 percent of U.S. direct investment in both Africa and Asia combined.[59]

In the developed countries, on the other hand, around 1968 more than half of U.S. direct investment was in manufacturing industries, and less than one-third in mining: Canada and Europe each accounted for nearly 45 percent of U.S. investment in developed market economies. U.S. direct investment seems to play a significant role in technologically dynamic and high-growth manufacturing industries.

Since the creation of the Common Market and with the convertibility of the European currencies, the flow of

direct investment has considerably increased. The flow of
U.S. direct investment might be associated with (not
necessarily causally related to) the rates of growth of a
number of European countries and it has been suggested
that "even the most cursory glance at the structure of U.S.
firms in Europe reveals that their activities are heavily
concentrated in two sectors: first, the science-based, the
research intensive, industries supplying both producer and
consumer goods, and second, industries subject to economies of scale and producing products with a high
income elasticity of demand."[60]

Servan-Schreiber has given an illustration of the nature
of the control of American corporations in the European
market: 15 percent in consumer goods, 50 percent in
semiconductors, 80 percent in computers, 95 percent in
integrated circuits. It has also been suggested that in 1965
U.S. investment in Europe was financed substantially
through European funds: 55 percent out of loans from the
European capital markets and direct credits from the
European countries, 35 percent out of local earnings and
subsidies from the European governments, and nearly 10
percent originated from the U.S. in the form of direct
dollar transfer.[61] Rolfe, on the other hand, has observed
that American subsidiaries in Europe are facing an increasing pressure of overcapacity.[62] Hymer and Rowthorn have
suggested that in the coming competition between U.S.
and European corporations, the market of the developing
countries will be an important battleground.[63]

In Canada, according to reports by *Newsweek*,[64]
Americans control more than 700 Canadian companies,
including more than half of the mining industry, 85
percent of the rubber industry, 75 percent of the transportation industry, and 75 percent of the petroleum industry.
In Australia, according to *The New York Times*,[65] the
directory of Australian industrial corporations issued by
the government indicates that nearly 1,000 companies
registered have substantial foreign ownership or control:
automobile assembling 88 percent; chemicals and pharma-

ceuticals 73 to 82 percent; production of nonferrous metal 84 percent; principal automobile manufacturing and oil exploration virtually 100 percent. U.S. direct investment is about $3.5 billion and at least one-third of manufactured goods exported are produced by firms with substantial U.S. ownership.[66]

The latter part of the twentieth-century world order seems to be characterized by the phenomenal growth of the multinational corporations which have had considerable influence in the developed countries. Some have argued that a major part of the world's production will be accounted for by 600 to 700 multinational corporations, that by around the year 2000 they will undertake more than 50 percent of total world production.[67]

There has been speculation made earlier that the rate of profit is not the primary determinant of the contemporary flow of direct private investment. Risk element might be an important factor. But it can also be noted that the developed countries offer easy access to a well-organized and well-developed capital market; that their high and rapidly growing per capita income offers a vast and expanding product market; that the availabilities of skills and the supporting infrastructure for modern production methods are more important than easy access to abundant unskilled labor and raw materials; that government policies might have created a favorable climate facilitating the growth of multinational corporations.

In the developed countries, a multinational corporation may be important but not necessarily crucial; at the same time the level of industrial development in these countries, their store of technical knowledge, availability of skills, and infrastructure all put the developed countries in a favorable position to benefit from the dynamic impacts of the multinational corporation. Whatever adverse effects arise from the behavior of a multinational corporation, the economies are strong enough to be able to absorb it. In the developing countries, on the other hand, a multinational corporation can become crucial to the economy, while at the same time the country concerned is merely marginal from the point of view of the corporation, giving it a considerable power and profound influence on the government. A multinational corporation can become a threat to the economic independence of a developing country.[68]

By its very nature, the multinational corporation strives for a global profit maximization strategy (although it may be subordinated to the needs for survival and power consolidation) and its decision making in this respect lies outside the jurisdiction of governments. While in the developed countries such a strategy may be consistent with the national interest, there is no reason to expect that the multinational corporation's strategy of global profit maximization will be consistent with the national development planning strategy of a developing country.

Given the state of technology, the backward and forward linkages of manufacturing industries may be very limited, the more so the lower the stage of industrialization in a developing country. It can be noted, for example, that partial assembling of integrated circuits in Hong Kong, Singapore, and Taiwan (the first two are the only industrialized developing countries, the last is already semiindustrialized) involves technological fragmentation, where imported parts are assembled locally and then exported for further processing. It is doubtful whether direct investment of such nature benefits the host countries technologically to a significant extent. In fact, it can be in the interest of the multinational corporation to import inputs from and to export outputs to parent companies or associated affiliates, which facilitates the adoption of one of the complex mix of remittance methods to transfer funds out of the host country and permits price manipulation (by charging higher prices on imported inputs and lower prices on exported outputs, thereby remitting profits and at the same time giving the appearance of low rate of profit).[69] Besides, an industry operating under such an arrangement will also be highly vulnerable to the vagaries of international finance, which is outside the control of the host country (such as the revaluation of currencies).

A subsidiary which considerably depends on input sources and output outlets on the parent companies or associated affiliates will make the host country vulnerable and its growth can be associated with increasing pressure on the balance of payments (enhanced by the flexibility in its price manipulation). It is not to be expected that the remittance of funds out of the host country will be adjusted to the country's balance of payments position, but rather it is more likely to be determined by the global needs of the multinational corporation and the opportunity costs of the funds elsewhere. Furthermore, it is not clear whether the net inflow of financial resources will in actuality be substantial: rather than complementing inadequate domestic financial resources, foreign corporations may be competing with local enterprises instead through short-term and long-term borrowing in the local money market.[70]

The vulnerability cannot be alleviated, nor can the potential benefits of the dynamics and efficiency of the multinational corporation be fully exploited by the host country, through a mere decree for larger participation and control by nationals. Joint ventures[71] with a weak partner cannot last long: unless its own interest dictates otherwise, the global resources of the multinational corporation will permit it to usurp from the initial local participation by deliberately operating at a loss (such a loss can be recovered in the long-term strategy, but it is disastrous to the local partners). Given the marginal status for a country from the viewpoint of a multinational corporation, what is a mere nuisance for the latter can be a trauma for the host country.

Thus, the issue of the multinational corporation in the developing countries is not one of excessive profits[72] or its exploitative nature, but rather it is a question of the vulnerability of the host country. The more vulnerable a country is, the more unhealthy will be the relation, and there will be more potential conflict and friction. It will be more likely that a host country will be the more vulnerable the less developed it is, which carries the implication that it will be entertaining a false hope that foreign direct investment will be the energizer for economic development.

Nor is it a question of ideology. In the centrally planned economies, socialist ideology precludes private ownership of the means of production. Accordingly, foreign capital inflows have taken more in the form of loans rather than equity capital. Foreign private corporations have entered into collaboration with a public firm in the host country, the former supplying services for which they are paid a fee as well as a share in the profits from sales. Jacoby has observed that the collaboration has not created a feeling of "exploitation" and that there even have appeared cracks in the ideological barrier; thus, for example, it has been noted that "the foreign investment law of Yugoslavia was amended during 1967 to permit joint ventures of Yugoslavian and foreign companies to acquire ownership of domestic fixed assets."[73]

In the developing countries, the type of financing of investment through foreign capital inflows (where the policy of the donors seems to limit official flows to the financing of social overhead and reserving directly productive investment for private capital flows) seems to be less favorable than the type which could be generally obtained by the presently developed countries through the international capital market during the nineteenth-century world order. The average annual rate of interest on bond issues in the nineteenth century was probably about 5 percent, but it is much higher now; aid and other loan capital are tied down with restrictions that could add to their real costs, and the terms of loan capital are harder; the tendency now is toward the preponderance of direct private investment, which involves an average rate of return considerably higher than interest on bond issues.[74] From the purely financial costs, bond issues are preferable to direct investment and other private capital borrowing (besides, there is an added advantage that compared to the unpredictable profits, dividends, and remittances, repayments and interests on bonds are known in advance); such an option, however, is not generally available and even if it is, will most likely be in the more developed developing countries. Japan is an example of a country where rapid technical progress can be attained without a significant inflow of direct investment but rather through the payments of foreign patents and licencing contracts.[75] Its initial conditions, however, are unlike those existing in even the most developed of the developing countries.

On the whole, arguments could be presented either way, that foreign capital inflow could accelerate or retard growth, could strengthen the economy or make it more vulnerable to outside forces. Much would probably depend on the inner strength of the economy, which determines the extent to which a developing country can exploit the potential benefits of foreign capital inflow, rather than being exploited by it. In any case efforts should be made to restrict its role to a complement of, rather than a substitute for, domestic resources. And inner strength cannot be achieved without a deliberate strategy toward self-reliance and the attainment of economic independence.

Population and GDP Growth

A problem regarding the growth of GDP can also be seen within the context of another variable, viz., the population in a given country. Access to domestic savings and external capital can be transformed into productive investment only if the required skill and organizational ability are available. The population of an economy assumes the dual role of a factor of production, and of a consumer. As a factor of production, population constitutes an economic base for realizing higher output. In its capacity as a consumer, population demands a share in the economy's output for the satisfaction of its needs.

From the production side, by defining average productivity of labor as the ratio of gross domestic product to employed labor force, the following relationship can be obtained: the rate of growth of gross domestic product is the sum total of the rate of growth of the employed labor force and the rate of growth of the average labor productivity. From such a relationship it can be seen that population increase could produce an increase in output provided that the population increase is also accompanied by a nonnegative sum total of growth rates of employed labor force and of labor productivity. If the rate of growth of gross domestic product refers to the maximum rate of growth of output that is consistent with the full employment of a growing labor population and the rising trend of labor productivity, such a growth rate can be referred to as the "socially optimal rate of growth." It can be noted that "the actual realization and maintenance of such a maximum rate of growth will be found to depend on there being the same rate of capital accumulation, thus implying a possible conflict between a desire for full employment (of labor) and a desire for higher consumption and a desire for higher savings."[76]

From the consumption side, if the standard of living is measured by per capita gross domestic product, the rate of growth of the standard of living will be equal to the difference between the rate of growth of gross domestic product and the rate of growth of population. In conjunction with the reference made earlier on the productive aspect of population, it can be seen that the rate of growth in the standard of living will be positive only if the rate of growth of the average labor productivity exceeds the difference between the growth rates of employed labor force and population.

In the developing countries, the acceleration in population growth has resulted in a rapid juvenescence of the population—efforts to increase literacy rates and educational levels have, therefore, been complicated by the upsurge in the school-age population. Expenditure on education has absorbed an increasing share of gross domestic product, particularly among the low-growth countries.[77] Accordingly, the increase in population in the developing countries may have prevented or slowed down the efforts to raise people to general levels of skill and organizational ability, particularly in the low-growth countries.

In the developing countries, rapid urbanization has accompanied population growth: between 1920 and 1960, rural and small town populations grew at about 1 percent a year, urban populations (defined as those living in communities of over 20,000 persons) by almost 4 percent a year, and big-city populations (of over 500,000 persons) by almost 6 percent.[78] As noted earlier, this rapid rate of urbanization cannot be interpreted as the normal concomitant of economic growth. Unless employment in the urban sector can grow corresponding to the rapid rate of urbanization, population growth with its consequent urbanization will simply result in increased urban unemployment. On the other hand, population growth might not be accompanied by increased rural employment as well, so that the general level of employment might continuously decrease.

The productive aspect of the normal population growth in some developing economies, at least in the short run, is suspect. On the other hand, population growth necessarily results in the increased demand for consumption. While population is a productive asset, it is also a liability: unless a developing economy can tolerate an unfavorable combination of production and consumption effects of population growth, the minimization of the growth rate of population is of practical necessity.

From the Malthusian viewpoint, the essence of the population problem is related to food shortage, which will ultimately reduce its growth. The consumption effect, on the other hand, suggests that population growth can lead to the concomitant decrease in savings and capital accumulation, thereby lowering per capita income. Some economists have suggested that underdevelopment can be explained in terms of the so-called "Malthusian trap" or "low-level equilibrium trap."[79] In the twentieth-century world order, however, growing mass unemployment engenders explosive social and political problems, which will surface long before mass starvation could lead to the natural decrease of population. The limit to the population growth rate is not particularly relevant as long as the economy can absorb its consequent increase in the working force, where population growth does not merely result in the growing number of mass unemployment.

NOTES

1. H. B. Chenery and A. M. Strout, *Foreign Assistance and Economic Development*, AID Discussion Paper No. 7 (revised), June, 1965, p. 4.
2. M. F. Millikan, *A Strategy of Development* (New York: United Nations, 1970), p. 10.
3. In the British economy, for example, exports until the depression period of 1873-96 grew faster than aggregate income: by the end of the eighteenth century exports had amounted to only about one-eighth of its national income and it reached more than one-fifth by the early 1870s. Foreign markets played a decisive role in some major industries, most notably in textiles where by the end of the nineteenth century almost four-fifths of the total value of output was exported, and iron and steel which from the mid-nineteenth century relied on foreign markets for about two-fifths of its gross production. Since Britain had virtual monopoly of industrialization in the context of an international vacuum, it was in the position to build and cultivate international trade to its advantage. The British hegemony in the presently advanced countries was temporary and soon eroding because of emerging competition; the hegemony over its colonies was long-lasting because of somewhat permanent complementary economies through the creation of economically dependent satellites. Although some colonial and semicolonial countries appeared to experience a burst of rapid export growth, the full impact of exports as an engine of growth

at the periphery was constrained only in those areas of European settlement. In others, however, exports growth resulted simply in their economies being enmeshed in a system of international division of labor which condemned them to specializing in the production of primary commodities.

4. In some developing countries, there have been remittances from temporary or permanent migrant workers, e.g., Algerians in France, Koreans in Japan, Mexicans in the United States.

5. Japan, for example, has relatively poor natural resources, but it has been able to achieve a high level of production as well as high rates in its growth.

6. See E. F. Denison, *The Sources of Growth in the United States and the Alternatives before Us* (New York: Committee for Economic Development, 1962), and his *Why Growth Rates Differ* (London: Allen and Unwin, 1968). See also J. Vaizey (ed.), *The Residual Factor in Economic Growth* (Paris: OECD, 1965), and M. Abramovits, "Economic Growth in the United States," *American Economic Review,* September, 1962.

7. The use of the production function approach in macroeconomic studies was pioneered by Charles Cobb and Paul Douglas; their function, widely known as the Cobb-Douglas production function, explains growth in terms of capital and labor inputs, but does not specify the productivity component (C. W. Cobb and P. H. Douglas, "A Theory of Production," *American Economic Review,* Supplement, March, 1928; P. H. Douglas, "Are There Laws of Production?" *American Economic Review,* March, 1948). Later studies for the developed countries have utilized the Cobb-Douglas function for the estimation of technical progress (for the developing countries, the function has also been used by emphasizing the role of capital or capital accumulation). Tinbergen was the first to treat technical progress explicitly as a separate variable in the aggregate production function through using an exponential time trend; his estimate of the rate of growth of the total factor productivity for the U.S. economy (1870-1914), which amounts to 1.1 percent per annum, is remarkably close to Schmookler's 1.09 percent per annum, also for the U.S. economy (1869-1938) but through utilizing the factor shares method (J. Tinbergen, "Zur Theorie der langfristigen Wirtschaftsentwicklung," *Weltwirtschaftliches Archiv,* May, 1942; J. Schmookler, "The Changing Efficiency of the American Economy, 1869-1938," *Review of Economics and*

Statistics, August, 1952; also S. Valavanis-Vail, "An Econometric Model of Growth, U.S.A., 1869-1953," *American Economic Association, Papers*, May, 1955). Kendrick's estimate, which includes longer series of data for the U.S. economy (1869-1953), is higher and amounts to 1.7 percent [J. W. Kendrick, "Productivity Trends: Capital and Labor," *Review of Economics and Statistics*, August, 1956, and his *Productivity Trends in the United States* (Princeton: N.B.E.R., Princeton University Press, 1961)]. Subsequently, rather than adopting the total productivity approach, attempts have been made to diminish the size of the productivity component by augmenting the estimates for factor inputs: the causes of growth are to be made more explicit through breaking down the total productivity into its various components. Fabricant, Abramovits, and Solow have observed that over the previous decades between 80 and 90 percent of the growth of output per head in the U.S. economy could not be accounted for by the mere increases in capital per head; Solow's estimate (as corrected by Hogan) suggests that about 90 percent of the rise in real output per man hour appears to be attributable to technical progress [S. Fabricant, "Economic Progress and Economic Change," *34th Annual Report of the National Bureau of Economic Research* (New York, 1954); M. Abramovits, "Resource and Output Trends in the United States Since 1870," *American Economic Association, Papers*, May, 1956; R. M. Solow, "Technical Change and the Aggregate Production Function," *Review of Economics and Statistics*, August, 1957; W. P. Hogan, "Technical Progress and Production Functions," *Review of Economics and Statistics*, November, 1958, and Solow's reply. See also B. F. Massel, "Capital Formation and Technological Change in U.S. Manufacturing," *Review of Economics and Statistics*, May, 1960, and H. S. Levine, "A Small Problem in the Analysis of Growth," *ibid.*]. The attempt to put the place of technical progress in perspective has produced controversies over whether the estimation of the rate of technical progress is to be based on embodied or disembodied hypothesis: the use of the Cobb-Douglas function has demoted the conventional hypothesis regarding the role of capital in the growth process, providing instead an overwhelming importance ascribed to the role of technical progress. Solow and Salter have both shown that technical progress is not an autonomous source of growth, but rather it makes its impact by being embodied in new capital. [R. M. Solow, "Investment and Technical Progress," in K. Arrow, S. Karlin, and P. Suppes (eds.), *Mathematical Methods in the Social Sciences* (Stanford: Stanford University Press, 1960), and his "Technical Progress, Capital Formation and Economic Growth," *American Economic Association, Papers,* May, 1962, and *Capital Theory and the Rate of Return* (Amsterdam: North Holland Publishing Co., 1963); W. E. G. Salter, *Productivity and Technical Change,* 2d ed. (Cambridge: Cambridge University Press, 1966). See also M. Abramovits, "Economic Growth," in B. Haley (ed.), *A Survey of Contemporary Economics,* Vol. II (Homewood, Ill.: Irwin, 1952); L. Johansen, "Substitution versus Fixed Production Coefficients in the Thoery of Economic Growth: A Synthesis," *Econometrica,* April, 1959; R. R. Nelson, "Aggregate Production Functions and Medium Range Growth Projections," *American Economic Review,* September, 1964].

Embodied models include those which specify that technical progress is a function of the rate of investment (N. Kaldor, "A Model of Economic Growth," *Economic Journal,* December, 1957) and of the cumulative investment, elaborated in Arrow's model of "learning by doing," where technical progress is completely embodied in new capital goods [K. Arrow, "The Economic Implications of Learning by Doing," *Review of Economic Studies,* June, 1962. Some consider learning as a function of time (N. Kaldor, "Comment on Professor Arrow's Paper 'The Economic Implications of Learning by Doing'," *ibid.*; W. A. Eltis, "Investment, Technical Progress and Economic Growth," *Oxford Economic Papers,* March, 1963) or of the rate of change of the investment rate (N. Kaldor and J. A. Mirrlees, "A New Model of Economic Growth," *Review of Economic Studies,* June, 1962). Denison, on the other hand, has considered that the embodiment hypothesis is not important (E. F. Denison, "The Unimportance of the Embodied Question," *American Economic Review,* March, 1964; also B. F. Massel, "Is Investment Really Unimportant?" *Metroeconomica,* April/August/December, 1962; E. Berglas, "Investment and Technological Change," *Journal of Political Economy,* April, 1965; D. W. Jorgenson, "The Embodiment Hypothesis," *ibid.,* February, 1966]. Regardless of whichever model is to be adopted, however, the results obtained through applied research seem to indicate that technical progress is the single most important, if not the prime, determinant of economic growth (see C. Kennedy and A. P. Thirlwall, "Technical Progress; A Survey," *Economic Journal*, March, 1972).

8. S. Kuznets, *Modern Economic Growth: Rate, Structure and Spread* (New Haven: Yale University Press, 1966).

9. While Solow suggested the concept of augmented capital input, Schultz stressed the important effects of education in order to regard it as a source of economic growth: education has now been considered as an investment in human capital and as a separate input in the aggregate production function, as well as an important factor to be considered in economic planning. [See T. W. Schultz, "Capital Formation by Education," *Journal of Political Economy*, December, 1960, and his "Investment in Human Capital," *American Economic Review*, March, 1961, *The Economic Value of Education* (New York: Columbia University Press, 1963); G. T. Becker, "Investment in Human Capital: A Theoretical Analysis," *Journal of Political Economy* (Supplement), October, 1962, and his *Human Capital* (New York: Columbia University Press, 1964); and Denison's *The Sources of Growth in the U.S.* See also R. Nelson, "Research and Economic Growth," in R. S. Philips (ed.), *The Goal of Economic Growth* (New York: Norton, 1962); M. Debeauvais, "The Concept of Human Capital," *International Social Science Journal*, Vol. XIV, No. 4, 1962; OECD, *Policies of Economic Growth and Investment in Education* (Paris: OECD, 1962), and *Planning Education for Economic and Social Development* (Paris: OECD, 1963); M. J. Bowman, "Schultz, Denison and the Contribution of 'Eds' to National Income Growth," *Journal of Political Economy*, October, 1964; Z. Griliches, "Research Expenditures, Education and the Aggregate Agricultural Production Function," *American Economic Review*, December, 1964; F. Harbison and C. A. Myers, *Education, Manpower and Economic Growth* (New York: McGraw-Hill, 1964); S. Bowles, *Planning Education Systems for Economic Growth* (Cambridge: Harvard University Press, 1969)].

10. See W. W. Rostow (ed.), *The Economics of Take-off into Sustained Growth* (London: Macmillan, 1963); his *The Stages of Economic Growth* (Cambridge: Cambridge University Press, 1960), and "The Take-off into Self-sustaining Growth," *Economic Journal*, March, 1956.

11. See A. Gerschenkron, *Economic Backwardness in Historical*

Perspective (Cambridge: Harvard University Press, 1961); G. Ranis and J. C. H. Fei, "A Theory of Economic Development," *American Economic Review*, September, 1961; W. A. Lewis, *The Theory of Economic Growth* (London: Allen and Unwin, 1959), and his "Economic Development with Unlimited Supplies of Labor," *Manchester School of Economic and Social Studies*, May, 1954; H. Leibenstein, *Economic Backwardness and Economic Growth* (New York: Wiley, 1957).

12. Myint, *op. cit.*, p. 51.

13. See also R. McKinnon, "Foreign Exchange Constraints in Economic Development and Efficient Aid Allocation," *Economic Journal*, June, 1964.

14. N. H. Jacoby, *An Evaluation of U.S. Economic Aid to Free China, 1951-1965*, AID Discussion Paper No. 11, 1966; H. B. Chenery and M. Bruno, "Development Alternatives in an Open Economy: the Case of Israel," *Economic Journal*, March, 1962. See also H. B. Chenery and A. MacEwan, "Optimal Patterns of Growth and Aid: The Case of Pakistan," *Pakistan Development Review*, Summer, 1966.

15. A. Maddison, *Economic Progress and Policy in Developing Countries* (New York: Norton, 1970), p. 59, which attempts to make a distinction between autonomous and policy-induced growth within the framework of Denison's model.

16. Myint, *op. cit.*

17. See, for example, *Programming Techniques for Economic Development* (United Nations publication, Sales No. 60.II.F.3) and *Studies in Long-term Economic Projections for the World Economy: Aggregative Models* (United Nations publication, Sales No. 64.II.C.2).

18. See K. K. Kurihara, *The Keynesian Theory of Economic Development* (New York: Columbia University Press, 1959).

19. Chenery and Strout, p. 21.

20. Strategies and policies have often been set within the context of economic projections which focus on the crucial role of foreign exchange availability as the limiting constraint to growth in the developing countries [Compare, for example, *Feasible Growth and Trade Gap Projections in the ECAFE Region* (United Nations publication, Sales No. E.69.II.F.8) to *Mobilisation of Domestic Capital* (United Nations publication, Sales Nos. 1953.II.F.2-4)]. Important and influential contributions were made by Millikan and Rostow when serious discussions on

the need for substantial foreign aid to finance economic development were underway in the mid-1950s. It is based on the concept that economic development involves a structural break from a stagnant to a self-sustained growth, requiring a sudden burst of effort which would be beyond the available domestic resources in most countries, but would be considered feasible with foreign aid through a decade or two [M. F. Millikan and W. W. Rostow, *A Proposal: Key to an Effective Foreign Policy* (New York: Harper, 1957), and U.S. Senate, Special Committee to Study the Foreign Aid Program, *The Foreign Aid Program: Compilation of Studies and Surveys* (Washington: U.S. Government Printing Office, 1957)]. Critics have argued that the proliferation of development planning documents reflects not so much the increased willingness to assume greater responsibility for development, but rather it is the effect of the aid agencies' imposition by making aid conditional upon planning. Thus, for example, it has been observed that "the objective that is common to most countries in the drafting of a national plan is to justify a claim for foreign aid." (R. Vernon, "Comprehensive Model-building in the Planning Process: The Case of the Less Developed Countries," *Economic Journal*, March, 1966, p. 59).

21. T. E. Weisskopf, "An Econometric Test of Alternative Constraints on the Growth of Underdeveloped Countries," *Review of Economics and Statistics*, February, 1972.

22. R. Nurkse, *Problems of Capital Formation in Underdeveloped Countries* (Oxford: Blackwell, 1955).

23. J. S. Duesenberry, *Income, Saving and the Theory of Consumer Behavior* (Cambridge: Harvard University Press, 1949), p. 57.

24. *Op. cit.*, chap. III.

25. See H. S. Houthakker, "An International Comparison of Personal Savings," *Bulletin of the International Statistical Institute*, Vol. XXXVIII, 1961, and his "On Some Determinants of Savings in Developed and Underdeveloped Countries," in E. A. G. Robinson (ed.), *Problems in Economic Development* (London: Macmillan, 1965). See also I. Friend and P. Taubman, "The Aggregate Propensity to Save: Some Concepts and Their Application to International Data," *Review of Economics and Statistics*, May, 1966; J. G. Williamson, "Personal Saving in Developing Nations," *The Economic Record*, June, 1968.

26. See T. Haavelmo, *The Econometric Approach to Development Planning* (Amsterdam: North Holland Publishing Co., 1965);

M. A. Rahman, "Foreign Capital and Domestic Savings: A Test of Haavelmo's Hypothesis with Cross-country Data," *Review of Economics and Statistics*, February, 1968; N. H. Leff, Marginal Savings Rate in the Development Process: The Brazilian Experience," *Economic Journal*, Sept., 1968. (see also note no. 40).

27. W. A. Lewis, *Development Planning* (New York: Harper and Row, 1966), p. 124. Some illustrative figures may be noted. In India, it was observed that only one million people were assessed income tax; in Mexico, around merely 50,000 of the six million farmers paid income tax; in Pakistan, only one-tenth of the 1 percent of the total population paid income tax [See, respectively, N. Kaldor, *Indian Tax Reform* (New Delhi: Ministry of Planning, 1956); I. M. de Navarrete, "Agricultural and Land Taxation," in A. T. Peacock and G. Hauser, *Government Finance and Economic Development* (Paris: OECD, 1965); M. Haq, *The Strategy of Economic Planning* (Karachi: Oxford University Press, 1963)].

28. Referring to Ghana, Guyana, India, Mexico, Sri Lanka, and Turkey [see N. Kaldor, *Essays on Economic Policy*, Vol. I (London: Duckworth, 1964)].

29. I. M. D. Little, "Tax Policy and the Third Plan," in P. N. Rosenstein-Rodan (ed.), *Pricing and Fiscal Policies* (Cambridge: MIT Press, 1964).

30. P. M. Hauser, "The Social, Economic and Technological Problems of Rapid Urbanization," in B. F. Hoselitz and W. E. Moore (eds.), *Industrialization and Society* (Paris: UNESCO, 1963).

31. *World Economic Survey*, 1967, Part One (United Nations document E/4488/Rev.1), p. 35.

32. See, for example, C. R. Frank, Jr., "Urban Unemployment and Economic Growth in Africa," *Oxford Economic Papers*, vol. 20, 1968; W. Elkan, "Urban Unemployment in East Africa," *International Affairs*, July, 1970.

33. C. Douglas-Home, "The Arms Sales Race," in *The Year Book of World Affairs*, 1969, p. 138.

34. Compared to the developed economies, equipment is generally more expensive and construction cheaper. The United Nations Economic Commission for Latin America, however, has observed that on the whole the price of capital goods in the region was higher than in the U.S.A. [see *A Measurement of Price Levels and the Purchasing Power of Currencies in Latin America 1960-62* (E/CN.12/653), March, 1963].

35. R. Bicanic, "The Threshold of Economic Growth," *Kyklos*, No. 1, 1962. See also his "Social Pre-conditions and Effects of Moving over the Threshold of Economic Development," *International Social Science Journal*, vol. XVI, no. 2, 1968.
36. See *Review of International Trade and Development*, 1970, p. 38, and "Mobilization of Resources for Development" (TD/B/C.3/75/Add.1).
37. *Review of International Trade and Development*, 1967 (United Nations publication, Sales No. E.68.II.D.4), p. 5.
38. *Ibid.*, 1970, pp. 25-26.
39. Chenery and Strout, *op. cit.*, pp. III-5-6.
40. K. B. Griffin and J. L. Enos, "Foreign Assistance: Objectives and Consequences," *Economic Development and Cultural Change*, April, 1970, p. 326. For further discussions on the negative association between the domestic savings rate and the rate of capital inflow, see K. B. Griffin, "Foreign Capital, Domestic Savings and Economic Development," *Bulletin of the Oxford Institute of Economics and Statistics*, May, 1970, and the discussion in the same journal, May, 1971. See also notes 25 and 26 above.
41. Griffin and Enos, pp. 317-18.
42. *Review of International Trade and Development*, 1967, p. 5.
43. J. N. Bhagwati, *Amount and Sharing of Aid* (Washington: Overseas Development Council, 1970).
44. A. Piatier, "The Transfer of Development Resources," in P. Lengyel (ed.), *Approaches to the Science of Socio-economic Development* (Paris: UNESCO, 1971).
45. "Foreign Assistance: Objectives and Consequences," p. 325.
46. W. I. Thorp, "Foreign Aid: A Report on the Reports," *Foreign Affairs*, April, 1970, pp. 569-70.
47. D. Goulet and M. Hudson, *The Myth of Aid* (New York: IDOC, 1971); T. Hayter, *Aid as Imperialism* (Baltimore: Penguin, 1971). It can also be noted that some studies have pointed out the high cost of aid to the recipient [see G. Myrdal, *The Challenge of World Poverty* (New York: Pantheon, 1970), pp. 352-55; M. Haq, "Tied Credits—A Quantitative Analysis," in J. H. Adler (ed.), *Capital Movements and Economic Development* (London: Macmillan, 1967); J. A. Pincus, "The Cost of Foreign Aid," *Review of Economics and Statistics*, November, 1963; A. Maddison, *Foreign Skills and Technical Assistance in Economic Development* (Paris: OECD, 1965)].

48. J. K. Galbraith, *The Affluent Society* (London: Hamish Hamilton, 1958), p. 140. Cf. the American edition published by Houghton Mifflin in 1958.

49. G. Myrdal, *Asian Drama* (New York: Pantheon, 1968), vol. I, preface, p. xii.

50. It has been suggested that if the U.S. were to match the earlier capital outflow from the U.K., in relation to its per capita income, the Marshall Plan would have had to have been carried out twice annually [A. K. Cairncross, *Home and Foreign Investment, 1870-1913* (Cambridge, 1953)].

51. In the 1930s, however, there were defaults on bond obligations in many countries [see C. Lewis, *The United States and Foreign Investment Problems* (Washington: Brookings, 1948)].

52. See C. Lewis, *America's Stake in International Investments* (Washington: Brookings, 1938).

53. See H. W. Singer, "The Distribution of Gains Between Investing and Borrowing Countries," *American Economic Review*, May, 1950.

54. See J. S. Furnivall, *Colonial Policy and Practice* (Cambridge, Cambridge University Press, 1948) and *An Introduction to the Political Economy of Burma* (Rangoon: People's Literature Committee and House, 1957). For an analysis of the working of the political-economic alliance against progress and national socioeconomic reconstruction, see P. Baran, "The Political Economy of Backwardness," *Manchester School of Economic and Social Studies*, January, 1952. See also F. Clairmonte, *Liberalism and Economic Development* (London: Asia Publishing House, 1960).

55. *World Economic Survey*, 1965 (United Nations publication, Sales No. E.66.II.C.1), p. 49. *Also Foreign Investment in Developing Countries* (United Nations publication, Sales No. E.68.II.D.2), and IBRD, *Annual Report*, 1968.

56. *Review of International Trade and Development*, 1970, pp. 24.25.

57. Kindleberger has suggested that the growth of large firms could take three forms, viz., the national firm with foreign operation; the multinational corporation; and the international corporation. The first is the case where the international division of a national firm could run its overseas operation which is still relatively small. In the second case the national firm becomes a parent company by opening up a branch, a subsidiary, or a joint venture in a foreign country with a limited degree of autonomy.

The third is a whole complex of organization which loses its national identity and owes loyalty to no one country. [See C. P. Kindleberger, *American Business Abroad; Six Lectures on Direct Investment* (New Haven: Yale University Press, 1969). Also *Foreign Ownership and the Structure of Canadian Industry: Report of the Task Force on the Structure of Canadian Industry* (Ottawa: Queens' Printer, 1968)]. Presently, however, even the larger corporations with their worldwide networks could still be identified by the country of origin of the parent company.

58. United States Department of Commerce, *Survey of Current Business,* October, 1971, pp. 32-33.
59. S. E. Rolfe and W. Damm, *The Multinational Corporation in the World Economy: Direct Investment in Perspective* (New York: Praeger, 1970).
60. J. H. Dunning, "Technology, U.S. Investment and European Economic Growth," in C. P. Kindleberger (ed.), *The International Corporation; A Symposium* (Cambridge: MIT Press, 1970), p. 149. See also V. N. Bandera and J. T. Whyte, "U.S. Direct Investment and Domestic Markets in Europe,' *Economia Internazionale,* February, 1968.
61. J.-J. Servan-Schreiber, *The American Challenge* (New York: Atheneum, 1968), pp. 13-14.
62. Capacity utilization was 90 percent in 1964; it declined to 87 percent in 1965 and 81 percent in 1967 (Rolfe and Damm, *op. cit.,* p. 34).
63. S. Hymer and R. Rowthorn, "Multinational Corporations and International Oligopoly," in Kindleberger (ed.), *The International Corporation,* p. 91.
64. April 17, 1972.
65. March 26, 1972.
66. Contained in an address by Ambassador W. I. Rice to the annual meeting of the American Chamber of Commerce in Australia as reported by *The New York Times,* March 26, 1972.
67. See A. Steiner and W. A. Cannon, *Multinational Corporate Planning* (New York: Macmillan, 1966), and S. Hymer, "United States Investment Abroad," paper presented to the Third Pacific Trade and Development Conference, Sydney, August, 1970.
68. See S. Hymer, *Direct Foreign Investment and the National Economic Interest,* Center Paper No. 108 (New Haven: Yale University Economic Growth Center, 1967). See also R. Ver-

non, *Sovereignty at Bay: The Multinational Spread of U.S. Enterprises* (New York: Basic Books, 1972).

69. For discussions on the financial aspect, see, for example, J. N. Behrman, *Some Patterns in the Rise of the Multinational Enterprise* (Chapel Hill: University of North Carolina, 1967); M. L. Brooke and H. L. Remmers, *The Strategy of Multinational Enterprises* (London: Longman, 1970); S. M. Robbins, D. M. Schydlowsky, and R. B. Stobaugh, *Money in the Multinational Enterprise: A Study of Financial Policy* (New York: Basic Books, 1972), and for the transfer of technology question, see, for example, Y. S. Chang. *The Transfer of Technology: Economics of Offshore Assembly—the Case of the Semiconductor Industry* (New York: UNITAR, 1971), and R. H. Mason, *The Transfer of Technology and the Factor Proportions Problems: the Philippines and Mexico* (New York: UNITAR, 1971). Much of what a multinational corporation would, or could, do in a developing country will probably depend on the nature of the industries concerned; the nature of the initial conditions relating to the local industries, such as whether or not they already attain the degree of efficiency capable of ensuring quality control and competitive prices for input supplies; the size of the domestic market and its importance to the multinational corporation setup; the options available to governments for exercising guidance or control; etc. In the case of India, for example, it has been noted that "one of the more dramatic examples of backward linkage is now under way in India, where IBM has applied for a license to produce its highly sophisticated 360 series. In doing so it has agreed to purchase the bulk of its components from local manufacturers, who must conform to the very high standards of quality and reliability inherent in this advanced technology." [S. E. Rolfe, *The Multinational Corporation*, Headline Series No. 199 (New York: Foreign Policy Association, 1970), p. 45]. Similarly, Brazil and Mexico have attempted the use of policies directed toward the gradual increase in the proportion of the domestically produced components for import-substituting and export industries. For Latin America in general, it has been argued that "between 1957 and 1966, there was an increase in the ties between United States-controlled subsidiaries and local suppliers, especially in automobiles and electronics. . . . In all likelihood, some of the new foreign-owned facilities were repeating the cycle of the older

investors, beginning with assembly or with packaging, eventually to become more deeply integrated in the economy." [R. Vernon, *Restrictive Business Practices; the Operations of Multinational United States Enterprises in Developing Countries* (United Nations publication, Sales No. E.72.II.D.16), p. 13].

70. As exemplified by the European experience. See also C. McMillan, Jr., R. F. Gonzalez, and L. G. Erickson, *International Enterprise in a Developing Economy* (East Lansing: Michigan State University, 1964).

71. For advantages and disadvantages of joint ventures, see, for example, Brooke and Remmers, *The Strategy of Multinational Enterprises*, and Kindleberger, *American Business Abroad*; see also J. M. Stopford and L. T. Wells, Jr., *Managing the Multinational Enterprise* (New York: Basic Books, 1972). Recently, Vernon has suggested that in terms of the economic advantages to the developing countries, "wholly-owned subsidiaries are probably a slightly more attractive bargain than joint ventures" (*Restrictive Business Practices*, p. 25). He has argued that when measured in absolute terms, the transfer of tangible and intangible resources associated with wholly-owned subsidiaries is more than that associated with joint ventures with the same general function: multinational enterprises place more capital in a wholly-owned subsidiary and are more ready to provide access to their worldwide distribution system as well as to their pool of technical and managerial resources. It has been argued further that in their relationships with the wholly-owned subsidiaries, parent companies appear more permissive and are more ready to waive royalties, to forego dividends, and to assign export markets to such entities; moreover, it has been suggested that dividend payments in relation to profits have tended to be a bit lower for wholly-owned subsidiaries than for joint ventures.

72. The relation between the host country and a multinational corporation can not necessarily be described by the zero-sum game, where the gain to one is a loss to another: both in effect participate in sharing the reward from monopoly or oligopoly, the amount of share being determined by the strength of the bargaining position of each. More important than the question of profit accrued to the multinational corporation is the issue of national interest defined within the framework of the long-term strategy of economic and social development: the issue to be crystallized is not how much profit has been extracted, but

rather, given alternative viable options in a given situation, whether the activities of the multinational corporation could be considered detrimental or beneficial to the national interest.

While generalization is dangerous, what is to be avoided is the premature plunging into the course of action which could lead a country further away from self-reliance and economic independence. A country should first decide, within the context of the long-term plan strategy and the deadweight of its historical inheritance, what projects it wants and when, and whether foreign participation would be required for such purpose within the given time dimension in order to make these projects viable; if foreign participation should be needed, whether viable options point out to the desirability of wholly-owned foreign enterprise, of entering into some degree of partnership, or of a mere management contract; in either of these forms of foreign participation, when the country ought to phase it out.

In the case of the multinational corporation, preoccupation with the profit being extracted by it appears to be a fruitless and frustrating exercise: the question of excessive or normal profit, given the inherent nature of the multinational corporation, covers an area whereby the multinational corporation and the host country could each provide legitimate claims, but still leave a considerable room for disagreement; even with the best of good-will on both sides, each could accuse the other of unfair practices. Normally a multinational corporation had at one stage experienced growth in its own home market, so that it enjoyed economies of scale and acquired a monopolistic or oligopolistic status: in the final analysis, differences in the rates of profit might be attributable to market imperfection or to the economies of scale factor, but it would not be easy to attribute it correctly in actual practice.

Leaving aside the question of whether profits are due to a monopolistic condition or to efficiency, the rate of profit itself is difficult to measure for a branch, subsidiary, or joint-venture unit of a multinational corporation in a given locality: it is determined by revenues obtained and costs incurred through the operation of such a unit, either one of which does not necessarily appear on the books of the given unit as international transactions between the units merely constitute an intratransaction within the multinational corporation. An attempt to measure the rate of profit is subject to a host of conceptual and operational difficulties in the face of the arbitrary nature of such an internal transaction with its consequent internal pricing: the parent company has at its disposal certain facilities such as the global lines of credit, marketing network, pool of organizational, managerial, and technological skills which could be shared by all its units, but its value to each could be assessed only arbitrarily; the crucial inputs might be supplied by other units operating outside the country in a system of a world-market oligopolistic structure (such as overseas research facilities for pharmaceuticals and technologically dynamic industries, nonsubstitutable components); the only market outlet of a unit might be other overseas vertically-integrated industries controlled by the same parent company (such as aluminum smelting, copper processing, oil refinery); etc. Furthermore, the distribution of profits among the units is subject to the constraint of the maximization of global profit, where the latter is under the discretion of the parent company whose decision is dictated by the special needs to show high or low profit for a given unit and not by the profit actually accrued to the given unit.

73. N. H. Jacoby, "The Multinational Corporation," *Center Magazine*, May, 1970, p. 47.

74. Probably about three-quarters of the foreign assets in the developing countries represent direct foreign investment. Some countries such as Argentina, Brazil, Ivory Coast, and Jamaica were able to raise bond issues in the international money market, which around the year 1968 cost about 8.5 percent.

75. The payments for foreign patents and licenses amounted to $177 million in 1966, four times the size of the dividend payments on direct foreign investment in Japan according to one estimate [A. Maddison, *Economic Growth in Japan and the USSR* (London: Allen and Unwin, 1969), p. 62]. Throughout the postwar years, Japanese firms entered into licensing contracts with foreign firms for which they paid an estimated sum of about $1.5 billion (Rolfe, *The Multinational Corporation*, p. 43).

76. Kurihara, *op. cit.*, pp. 45-46.

77. Cf. *World Economic Survey*, 1967, Part One, Table 13.

78. Cf. *World Social Situation*, 1967 (United Nations publication, Sales No. E.68.IV.9), p. 14.

79. Leibenstein, *op. cit.*

CHAPTER III

SECTORAL ASPECT
OF GROWTH

The preceding chapter discussed the main determinants of income growth within the confines of an aggregative framework. While there are controversies over the extent of its role, capital accumulation or investment seems nevertheless to be an important determinant of growth. According to the aggregative model, *any* increase in investment that does not result in a fall in its productivity below a minimum acceptable level and that accelerates growth is justifiable. Given two alternative growth paths resulting from a given investment, the one that will yield the higher growth rate is preferable to the one that produces the lower one. Such a conclusion is inevitable if one merely considers the quantitative aspect of growth or if one prefers to regard quantifiable growth as the supreme goal to which all else should be subordinated.

The stereotyped description of a developing country is the land where the war against poverty, hunger, disease, and ignorance has to be fought. In this war, growth is urgent and the developing countries are desperate. One could smell the air of wretched poverty if he happens to encounter the despair of the undernourished peasant who toils the land from sundown to sunset for a meager subsistence, wearing unwashed and torn rags as his only clothing; or the filth of shantytowns populated by working-age men whose only certainty is the uncertainty of how to earn a living; etc. But in the same land one could also witness luxurious rarities even in the most developed of nations, such as extravagantly lavish champagne parties attended by impeccably dressed local elite (and brilliantly bejewelled ladies), transported in the latest immaculate sedans and limousines; spectacular villas with gardens as large as the eye can see; luxurious casinos, nightclubs, amusement and entertainment places; etc.

Growth that makes the rich richer and the poor poorer is not an indisputable goal. Not every type of growth is desirable. Some economists would argue that quantity is a luxury to be considered only after the quality problem is solved. That is a value judgment. The question of goal is not free from value judgment. Growth that makes the rich national elite richer at the expense of the poor is an affront to social justice; if the rich person is a foreign resident, it raises the issue of what independence is all about.

Even without dwelling on social justice and other philosophical issues, the desirability of growth that maintains or worsens the structure of underdevelopment is questionable. Growth without being accompanied by a corresponding structural transformation but which attenuates the structure of underdevelopment is shortsighted.

In practice, therefore, the strategy and policy for economic development cannot be based solely on the quantitative aspect of growth alone. Developing countries are characterized (though in different degrees) by external dependence and vulnerability, structural weaknesses and dualism, with sectoral dislocations and disparities in productivity, where growth has not been primarily generated by the internal dynamics of its own but more the result of the act of nature or the diffusion process from outside. Developing countries are the victim of the nineteenth-century world order which had facilitated a certain type of division of labor to occur, viz., specialization in the production and exports of primary commodities, on the one hand, and market for manufactured goods, on the other. This aspect has become very familiar in the literature on economic development, but so are the attempts, in the very distant past as well as most recently, to justify such a type of international division of labor on the ground that the developing countries' comparative advantage lies in the bounty of their natural resource endowments and accordingly they would be better off to follow the "efficient" pattern.

Such perverted doctrine had deflected the developing countries into the types of economic activity that is devoid of its own internal dynamics. The three distinguishable thresholds that coincide with different industrial revolutions had been a remote experience: the native inhabitants had been robbed of sectoral activities which offer the scope for technical progress. Thus, while the twentieth-century world order is characterized by intense technological progress, which considerably improves the vast accumulated knowledge and acquired experience of the past, and when technical progress has become the significant contributing factor to growth, the native inhabitants have neither had the store of knowledge nor the acquired experience (relevant within the context of their own nationally integrated production requirements) corresponding to what had been known and adapted during the preindustrialization phase of the contemporary advanced countries.

Nor do the developing countries have, again within the context of their own nationally integrated production requirements (and also in different degrees that accord to their different stages of development), a sufficiently well-developed human, physical, and financial infrastructure. A country may have a considerably high literary rate and a great number of its citizens may be able to elegantly recite Shakespeare and Voltaire, but the literates are inept when it comes to the directly productive activities. An excellent road may connect certain points in the countryside to the harbor with excellent port and storage facilities; yet, in the

same country, famine in one region can coexist with an
oversupply of food in another which becomes rotten
because there is no means for interregional transportation.
Scarcity of financial resources can exist in the face of an
increasingly larger outflow of indigenous capital or more
bank accounts abroad. Transport and communication,
organizational network of finance, insurance, banking and
credit facilities, trade and commerce, tax systems, etc., are
not necessarily geared to the main domestic economic
activities, but rather, fashioned to the requirements of the
intercourse with advanced countries. Even the educated
elites are not necessarily rooted to their own culture and
tradition.

The structure of underdevelopment is fundamental and
it has facets each of which assumes an important proportion and could lead to fallacious solution. Once in a while
there have emerged ideas advocating policies based on
some new discovery of the notion of the cause of underdevelopment which on further reflection may turn out to
be a mere symptom. For example, the cause of underdevelopment is a lack of skill: thus the solution is manpower
planning to increase the supply of skills even when there is
no clear idea whether the domestic economic activities will
generate the demand for such an increase in skills. Or else
it is due to lack of industrialization: thus vigorous import
substitution and a country will then take pride in its
progress for being able to produce automobiles even when
the simplest screws and bolts would have to be imported,
or even when the size of the market is very small (with no
prospect for its immediate increase) as to result in chronic
underutilization of capacities in the production structure.
Or it is due to lack of infrastructure: thus the construction
of highways and bridges even with a very low load factor.
Or it is due to lack of foreign exchange: thus concentration on export activities even when the commodities are
subjected to more and more technological obsolescence.
And so on, and so on.

Obsession with the endeavor to discover the cause of

underdevelopment, if it merely leads to the compartmentalization of the development problem, could yield a prescriptive panacea, which in fact is a mere simplistic solution and could even defeat the whole purpose of development effort. The uprooting of the fundamental structure of underdevelopment requires a total and concerted effort, defined within an overall development strategy. Growth is necessary, and important, but it is not everything and not all that matters. Growth needs to be defined within the context of self-reliance and a greater economic independence strategy. Self-reliance means that growth is generated primarily by internal forces and capabilities, and is an integral part of the process that meets internal needs. Greater economic independence means that growth is the product of the establishment of greater internal interdependencies, structural as well as regional, permitting the growth to be propelled by the economy's own internal dynamics. Growth without self-reliance and greater economic independence can be thwarted by the decline in external stimulant and injection; if the economy has thus become an addict, it has an incurable disease of external vulnerability.

The strategy of self-reliance and greater economic independence is not autarchic, nor is it isolationistic. A self-reliant and economically independent economy can become an active and vigorous trading partner in the world economy, for self-reliance and independence do not preclude healthy and strong interdependence.

It is because the structure of underdevelopment is a fundamental problem that progress in its attenuation is difficult to measure. Underdevelopment is a relative concept: a given state of underdevelopment in the face of rapid development in other countries can be considered as a growing underdevelopment. In the developed economies the growth in per capita GDP can be interpreted as the manifestation of development; such a growth rate is a convenient measure of their development performance and there are generally agreed computational methods (although, as will be discussed in another chapter, what is thus being computed is much less clear in regard to the developing countries). In the developing countries, on the other hand, the growth in per capita GDP can occur within the structure of growing underdevelopment. That growth in the developing countries has generally been considered as development seems to be based on mere presumption and there does not seem to be any reason to suppose that it is analytically founded. It is, however, not innocently harmless, but could become misleadingly damaging. Higher growth rate with less self-reliance and greater economic dependence does not indicate better development performance compared to lower growth rate but with greater self-reliance and less economic dependence.

Some developing countries have already had a strong base and foundation to afford them in concentrating on other areas in the construction of the economic edifice; some others have yet to construct the foundation from scratch. A developing country that concentrates on building a strong base and foundation can be made a subject of the ridicule of failure as it is put in comparison to some glittering example of progress which within a short time span can already show the erection of an economic edifice (although in the longer run the latter may crumble).

As technical progress in the advanced countries tends to bring comparative advantage based on natural resources and local unskilled labor into technological obsolescence, the role of the developing countries pursuing this line of specialization in the world market has become less and less important. On the other hand, technical progress has also produced a pattern of consumption (and investment) that has made imports from the advanced countries more and more indispensable. These alone would be enough to exert increasing pressure on the balance of payments but in addition, there are, for example, mounting interest and debt payments, indigenous capital outflow, profits and dividend remittances, etc. While development is a long-term problem, the developing countries have at the same time to cope with crises in the short term, where one of the principal sources is the balance of payments. Long-term strategy can accordingly be easily deflected by short-term crises.

In countries with rich natural resources and where the prospect for becoming the victim of technological obsolescence is not yet in sight, there are still options for a resources-induced type of growth. Lucrative profits can still induce vigorous private foreign investment. Revenues from exports might still be more than sufficient to redress the problems arising from underdevelopment. Fancy buildings and other signs of modernization in the capital can still be flourishing. Accelerated growth in GDP can occur without much effort and camouflaging the structure of growing underdevelopment.

Some other developing countries, however, are not as fortunate and even if they are, are no longer content with a mere growth in GDP unaccompanied by product diversification and structural transformation. Growth is no longer merely a quantitative question; rather, it touches upon a qualitative aspect: what kind of growth, how has it occurred, and who bears its costs and reaps its benefits—all has thus emerged as an important issue.

Difficulties confronting exports of primary products (and the deteriorating terms of trade) began to surface in the 1920s and were further compounded by the Great Depression. The Second World War cut off many developing countries from the supplies of manufactures and the outlets for primary commodities. Aggravated balance of payments crises led to import and foreign exchange restrictions, in effect creating a protected market for emerging local industries. Adversities and the growing recognition to external vulnerability have given impetus to industrialization policy. Since imports have had immediately visible markets, it is easiest to concentrate on import substitution during the initial phase. Import substitution has accordingly characterized industrialization policies of many developing countries.

At the sectoral level, industrialization has been considered the key to economic growth. While within the aggregative context, as discussed in the preceding chapter, foreign capital inflow has been regarded as a determinant of accelerated growth, within the sectoral framework, for well over a quarter of a century, industrialization through import substitution has been taken as a powerful tool for the task of achieving accelerated growth. On the other hand, there has been a growing recognition of the undesirability of putting too much emphasis on industrialization at the neglect of agriculture; increasing attention to agriculture has further been enhanced by the prospect for greater agricultural productivity because of the so-called Green Revolution.

Emphasis on industrialization alone, or on agriculture alone, is one form of compartmentalization and without the framework of an overall strategy, it can lead to undesirable consequences. While the nature of demand in industry permits its growth at a more accelerated rate than in agriculture, self-reliance and economic independence would require that the two sectors be made complementary with increasing mutual feedbacks to reach structural interdependence and integration; the growth of enclaves within and between the sectors is, therefore, not compatible with the strategy of self-reliance and economic independence.

The problem of technological obsolescence looms large, whether it is in industry or agriculture. Antiquated labor-intensive technique may be so inefficient that modern and capital-intensive technique can still require less capital per unit of output. However, modern methods evolving in the advanced countries are the response to their own particular factors scarcities and factors availabilities, which need not be similar to the existing conditions in the developing countries. Furthermore, modern methods do not necessarily involve the most up-to-date capital: what has become obsolete in the developed economies may still be economically useful in the developing countries, given the limited market size and relative factors scarcities in the latter.[1] Few developing countries have embarked upon the production of capital goods to a significant level (Argentina, Brazil, India, Mexico). On the other hand, some capital goods may be better produced in the developing countries, permitting specification and design to be tailored after factors availabilities and scarcities in the developing countries, which is hard to attain when the capital goods are mass-produced.[2] Production of simple capital goods and implements for the agricultural sector is also one form of industrialization.

The primary ingredient for self-reliance and economic independence is increasing mobilization and productive utilization of indigenous resources, involving greater participation of the larger populace in production activities. Industrialization through import substitution and the Green Revolution are not necessarily the catalyst for greater utilization of indigenous resources; in fact, they may merely generate a pattern of growth which increasingly displaces the role of certain indigenous resources (notably local unskilled labor) with imported inputs, and a switch-over in the distribution of income at the expense of the masses. The economy could even become externally more dependent and vulnerable in the face of such a pattern of growth.

Needless to say, accelerating the growth of industry and agriculture needs financing. It can be recalled that foreign capital inflow may be complementary or competitive to domestic savings; in any event, a greater part of the growth has to be financed from domestic sources. Since agricultural share is the larger the less industrialized a developing country is, it may be expected that agriculture would be the main source of financing industrialization. It can also be argued that given the assumption of redundant labor in the developing countries, the manufacturing sector should be subsidized or protected since it has to pay wages to labor whose social-opportunity cost in agriculture is zero.[3]

On the other hand, organizational and institutional aspects as well as technological backwardness in agriculture may be such that investible funds generated by this sector would not even be sufficient to finance its own modernization. Furthermore, labor is not the only factor of production in agriculture. The small peasants who toil the land are paying rent to landlords, usurious interest to money-lenders, and exorbitant profits accrued to middlemen and traders; insofar as these landlords, money-lenders, middlemen, and traders are urban consumers, there has been considerable urban exploitation even in the absence of industrialization. (The rate of urban exploitation becomes greater as protected industrialization increases prices of commodities needed by the peasant, and the more so if government interference facilitates continuously deteriorating terms of trade against agriculture.) Regardless of whether or not labor is abundant, there can be considerable urban exploitation of the agricultural sector to subsidize industry; Viner,[4] for example, has remarked on the urban exploitation of the rural sector in thinly populated countries.

A sector which is being given priority over others can expand only by attracting scarce resources from the rest of the economy, unless reorganization facilitates more productive utilization of previously idle resources (for example, reorganization in the agricultural sector may increase investible funds without the mass of the peasants having to lower their present consumption). Premature plunging into import substitution in all kinds of manufacturing production which the country is nominally able to produce may merely increase the general level of prices: inflation will then make trading and speculation activities more attractive than engaging directly in physical production. Industrialization would in this case ultimately lose its own momentum, benefiting no one except perhaps the privileged industrialists and those connected with trading and speculation, but it would be costly to the economy.

Self-reliance and a greater degree of economic independence strategy is, therefore, not a mere empty slogan: it frames the sense of perspective through looking at the economy's own inner strength. Accelerated growth promises pie in the sky, but there might still be some wisdom in tidying up one's present backyard. The promise of foreign aid and the lure of the dynamic impact of private foreign capital inflows have diverted attention to external forces and put too much emphasis on the mechanics of economic development (with the consequent imputing of all blames of failures to foreigners), rather than introspectively looking inward and regarding development as a complex process, which is an intricate interrelationship between the initial conditions, the mechanics of economic development, and the policy and strategy for economic development.

The backbone of many developing countries is agriculture and one may argue that its archaic production structure and the exploitative clutch of land tenure, marketing, and credit systems are not only interrelated, but they also result in the lack of effective demand to support mass-based industrialization. The lack of industrialization is in this case not the cause of underdevelopment but a mere symptom: uprooting the cause of underdevelopment will go into deeper and more fundamental problems than the simple increase in the number of factories located in a country.

Development has to be financed, and in the process some classes of society or some regions of a country are subsidizing its financing. During the nineteenth-century world order only few of the presently industrialized countries were not dependent to a substantial degree on colonial territories or spheres of influence (for markets of manufactured products, sources of inputs, and areas for further investment); in addition there was also class exploitation on the domestic scene. Japan is a country that has often been cited in the economic literature as a model of an underdeveloped country able to finance its own development without foreign aid but through the transfer of resources from agriculture. Japanese feudalism was ended by the Meiji reforms and a market economy subsequently developed with a very high land tax: the government in the Meiji era, however, extended protection to the consolidation of the landlord-tenant system.

Mexico has been considered as a developing country able to engage in a relatively efficient path of industrialization while recognizing the importance of agricultural expansion: thus its success is attributable to the whole development effort rather than to a simple one-sided concentration on industrialization. Despite land reforms, however, the government has done remarkably little in affecting the distribution of income; the distribution of income is very inequitable even by Latin American standard. Unequal personal and regional distribution of output and income in Brazil can also be observed despite its rapid industrial growth.

Pakistan has been well acclaimed as a model of a developing country that started from a very low level of per capita income and was able to accelerate its growth in GDP through the use of foreign capital inflows. The high cost of its industrialization is comparable to India, but it was able to expand exports of manufacturing products. Rapid growth in agriculture during the 1960s (attributable to the Green Revolution) is also the contributing factor in its overall growth performance, not merely the industrialization policy. Failure to achieve concrete results in removing the disparity in the income distribution contributed to the regional problem which tormented Pakistan; the acclamation of growth success has turned out to be premature in view of the subsequent national catastrophe.

The twentieth-century world order has given rise to the need for inward-looking development strategy. So far it seems that class subsidy for development financing could manage to be longer-lasting than regional subsidization. However, it does not preclude the possibility that today's apparent success as measured by growth, but one that widens the regional and personal income disparity, could eventually become a national catastrophe. Development is a total, concerted, and integrated effort involving structural integration as well as regional interdependence, where growth is important but is merely a subordinate question. Compartmentalization of the development problem or a superficial glossing over the aggregate are most likely to be fallacious. What is needed, is a pragmatic approach fashioned after the initial conditions of a particular country rather than a dogmatic and generalized treatment.

It can also be noted that a sudden or revolutionary change from the existing order, or drastic prevention from an undesirable path, in one way or another, will disrupt production performance, involve considerable economic costs, and require a political structure strong enough to absorb the consequence of possible social turbulence. To some degree, Japan's changeover from the Tokugawa system, Soviet collectivization, agrarian reforms in Bolivia, Cuba, and Mexico, China's Cultural Revolution, and various land reforms and nationalization measures adopted in some countries are examples. Only history can tell whether their consequent disruptive effects in production are in fact a contribution to their subsequent economic development.

On the other hand, half-way measures can also be disruptive. Hesitation over reforms has acted as a disincentive, its uncertainty inhibiting investment and stimulated private capital outflow. The fear of the possibility of land reforms would result in insecurity regarding the existing land tenure system, preventing efforts which might have otherwise increased agricultural productivity. In some cases, implementation of land reform has resulted in dissipation of land and capital assets, where the new structure produces economically too small units, lowering productivity or preventing its possible improvement.

Industry

Import Substitution

In the nineteenth-century world order, most of the presently developed countries had access to outlets for manufactured exports (as well as cheap sources of inputs and accumulated extracted surpluses) in privileged and protected markets in the colonies or spheres of influence. Some smaller European countries were contiguous to the larger ones and their manufacturing exports had relatively easy marketing access. Colonialism is presently out of the question and the developing countries, instead of having their own spheres of influence, are themselves the spheres of influence. When the contemporary developing countries started their industrialization (in Latin America it began in the 1930s), there were no cheap sources of inputs and surpluses other than their own, and technological progress elsewhere had advanced very rapidly while markets for manufacturing exports were not readily accessible (even in simple manufactured goods where the comparative advantage lies in the developing countries but which threatens domestic interest in the advanced countries).

During the 1930s, the world order was characterized by contracting international markets and trade restrictions. The cutting-off of manufacturing supplies in the Second World War and rising manufacturing prices in the late 1940s had given impetus to industrialization, especially in Latin America. Furthermore, there was gloomy pessimism regarding the export prospect and the growing recognition that reality was undermining the outdated scheme of the international division of labor.[5] In other developing countries, attempts at industrialization have followed the tide of independence.

Balance of payments difficulties have also produced protective measures, often in an *ad hoc* manner but at any rate they created protected markets for import substitutes. Industrialization activities which followed are not necessarily the results of carefully considered and well-planned programs, but rather they could be the mere response to *ad hoc* protective measures. The protective measures usually adopted are direct government control and quantitative restrictions, tariffs, and multiple exchange rates. In the discussion of the costs of industrialization, there has been a customary distinction between the *nominal rate of protection* (based on comparison of prices of products) and the *effective rate* (on a value-added basis).[6] Depending on the relationship between input and output, the effective rate can be considerably larger or smaller than the nominal rate; several country studies have reported negative protection as seen from the effective rate. Needless to say, that protected market which increases domestic prices can grossly exaggerate the value of the manufacturing share in GDP.

While in some developing countries industrialization has been the response to *ad hoc* protective measures, in others protection has been adopted deliberately to promote industrialization through import substitution. Some economists have suggested that import substitution enlarges domestic market. Myrdal has argued as follows:

> One of the difficulties of industrial development in [the developing] countries, and one of the great hindrances to giving real momentum to a development policy, is that internal demand must be built up simultaneously with supply. The unlikelihood or, anyhow, the exasperating slowness of any self-engendered process of "natural growth" offers a main explanation why sustained stagnation becomes a sort of natural equilibrium and why policy interventions are called for . . . import restrictions afford a means of by-passing altogether the process of "natural growth" and creating at once the necessary demand for a particular domestic industry. They create a sizeable internal demand for a specific commodity, without the necessity of waiting for the slow and difficult growth of the entire economy.[7]

And Hirschman has advocated that

> . . . imports still provide the safest, incontrovertible proof that the market is there. Moreover, they condition the consumer to the product, breaking down his initial

resistance. Imports thus reconnoitre and map out the country's demand; they reduce uncertainty and reduce selling costs at the same time, thereby bringing perceptibly closer the point at which domestic production can be economically started.[8]

In practice, the incipient manufacturing industries often engaged primarily in the import substitution of nondurable or light consumer goods, involving simple processing activities. These "finishing touches" industries import not only capital goods, but also semiprocessed or even almost completely processed materials, so that even a low rate of protection for the final product can produce a considerably higher effective protection. Domestic value added consists mostly of the wages for the workers in these "finishing touches" industries with no further linkages to the domestic sector. Such a type of industrialization policy will bring the economy into a more vulnerable position and to greater external economic dependence, the more so the less there is of the possibility for developing industries to produce substitutes for imported inputs: the banning of the import of finished products because of balance of payments difficulties is relatively easier compared to the stoppage of the imports of these inputs since the latter will have further repercussions arising from domestic resources having been committed to industries affected.

Industrialization through import substitution can lead a country to losing its sense of priority. If industry has priority over other sectors, the question is which types of industries are to be given priority over others. Once import-substituting industries have been established, economic policies could be shaped by the requirements of these industries, rather than have such industries adjust to the needs of the economy; thus, for example, difficulties in the balance of payments could cut down other more important imports simply to prevent these industries from closing down, no matter how uneconomic these might be and how unfounded their initial establishment had been. The problem will of course arise in any type of industrialization through import substitution, in durables and nondurables alike, as long as the industries established as its result are crucially dependent on imported inputs and there is no possibility for further substituting the imported inputs. While import substitution has less problem of creating demand as noted above, there is the question of whether the demand pattern as manifested by the import pattern is in fact representing the path which industrialization should follow. Many imported goods are only for a small minority of high-income groups where their domestic markets can easily be exhausted before production can even reach the point which can be justified economically: industrialization along this line does not produce its own momentum and removes sources of revenues from import duties.

According to Marcus Fleming, if the supplies of labor, capital, and other inputs are not perfectly elastic, the simultaneous establishment of a group of light consumer goods industries will be likely to result in external diseconomies for each other (through their competition for these limited resources), which will also be likely to outweigh the external economies that this group of industries is to generate for itself.[9] Fleming has suggested that a vertical grouping of industries at different stages of production where these industries become each other's customers or suppliers, might generate more economies.

It may well be that the relevant question to be asked in industrialization is not what items in the import bill a country would be physically able to produce (especially if the import content of import substitution would be likely to remain high), but rather which lines of production (previously imported or not) would be most likely to offer the prospect for greater national interdependence, structural and regional, so that the production system becomes more nationally integrated and less externally vulnerable, and the economy approaches self-reliance and achieves

greater economic independence. Infant industry and protection arguments can be used to promote industrialization, but the arguments do not justify the exploitation of
the nonindustrial sector to support industries where the
demand is very limited since it caters only to a very small
minority of the population, and where the input requirements constitute very large leakages abroad. Import substitution could lead to policies covering too broad an area
where the economy's scarce resources are spread too
thinly, where the superficial industrial structure could be
maintained only by undue permanent reliance on protective measures and on continuous supplies of imported
inputs.

Industrialization and Its Justification

The decade of the 1970s will most likely be characterized by a greater number of developing countries pursuing the goal of industrialization. Specialization in
primary commodities is a relatively simpler course compared to the complexity of engaging in industrialization,
but its complexity is at the same time offering the
prospect for dynamism.

Given the nonhomogeneous nature of the developing
countries, not everyone of them could follow the same
course of industrialization. Much will depend on the size
of the country, natural resources endowments, basic skills,
and entrepreneurship.

Some countries have the advantage of rich natural
resources which permit the development of industrial
activities related to resource exploitation, or have accordingly obtained financial resources to finance manufacturing industries (Malaysia, Venezuela, Zaire, Zambia). Some
small countries are also lacking in primary natural
resources; these countries are thus forced to adopt export-
oriented industrialization aimed at manufacturing exports to the world market (Hong Kong, Singapore).
Some had concentrated on import substitution and their

domestic markets were relatively large enough to permit their transition from a nonindustrial or an industrializing stage into becoming semiindustrialized developing countries (Brazil, India, Mexico). Some had followed the trend of import substitution in the 1960s, but subsequently concentrated on export markets or at least have begun to exploit their potentials (Brazil, Colombia, India, Israel, Mexico, Pakistan, Singapore, South Korea, Taiwan).

In industrialization programs, especially those based entirely on import substitution, efficiency consideration will be an adversary as well as an ally for decision making, depending on the time horizon present. The technological inferiority of the developing countries will almost certainly result in the incipient manufacturing industries being established to be inefficient by the standard of the world market: too much obsession with efficiency consideration will never get an industrialization program off the ground. On the other hand, complete disregard of efficiency consideration may also mean that the nonindustrial sector would have to bear the cost in subsidizing a high-cost industrialization program. As the vast majority of the indigenous population in the developing countries is in the nonindustrial sector while protections and incentives benefit not only indigenous industrialists but also foreign enterprises, complete disregard of efficiency consideration will give rise to an issue of whether the majority of the indigenous population should continuously sacrifice and subsidize the privileged beneficiaries composed only of the tiny minority of indigenous industrialists and foreign enterprises. It can be noted that the main attractions of establishing subsidiaries in import-substituting industries might not only be the high tariffs and other privileges but also the cheap unskilled labor for simple processing: an import-substitution industrialization program could merely result in the establishment of enclave industrial enterprises with direct linkages to the parent companies and very little to the domestic sector.

Temporary disregard of efficiency to promote industrialization could be justified because manufacturing industries possess characteristics which are unlike those of the agricultural sector. The developing countries had been robbed of sectoral activities which could generate their own internal dynamics: industrialization could transform the nature of the economy, make it more nationally integrated, more flexible and able to attain accelerated self-reliant growth resulting in greater economic independence, characterized by dynamism and modernization for its ability to generate indigenous managerial and entrepreneurial talent, technical skills, technological innovation, and rising productivity. The demand for manufacturing goods is more elastic than that for agriculture and thus its possible expansion is less affected by market constraints, facilitating more rapid growth than might have been possible otherwise, consequently generating increased demand for employment and offering the prospect for increased contribution of indigenous resources in production activities. Growing availability of manufactured goods produced along the lines which yield competitive cost structure offers the possibility for more export diversification, at the same time easing the balance of payments pressure and making the economy less vulnerable. In many developing countries the import trade has been in the hands of foreigners; the latter's role might be displaced by indigenous industrialists. In any case, the emerging monopolistic or oligopolistic class of industrialists might be preferable to the corresponding class of traders under the import regime: profits from trading are less likely to be invested in manufacturing enterprises, so that import substitution may initiate the process which encourages the emergence of a class of entrepreneurs whose outlook is completely different from the traditional traders' mentality. In any case, growing industrialization could lead to increasing investible funds.

Although there are advantages to be derived from industrialization, it cannot be presumed that simple protective measures will produce industrialization which will necessarily evolve toward the country's best advantage. Industrialization which is not explicitly geared to achieving greater interdependencies (structural and regional, within industry as well as between industry and agriculture) will hardly be likely to generate sustained dynamism. On the other hand, even if greater interdependencies could be obtained, the neglect of the country's own internal forces and capabilities as well as its divorce from the internal needs of the masses could thwart its further growth unless the country could rely on the world market. The possibility of the expansion of import-substituting industries catering merely to the high-income group is limited. A small country directly embarking upon the manufacture of passenger cars, refrigerators, and air conditioning, for example, will most likely not attain its own internal dynamism, export diversification of manufactures, will soon face market constraint and underutilized capacities, and will be crucially dependent on imported inputs. Much will, therefore, depend on the country's strategy and policy for economic development, its outlook, the political and social organization, the size and resources of the country. Protection programs are merely supportive measures; the support still needs further instruments of government controlling, prodding, interfering, cajoling the course of industrialization, so that the available scarce resources can be utilized to the best advantage of the country as a whole and not merely the sectional interest thereof. Industrialization, therefore, should be an integral part of the overall policy and strategy for economic development, and cannot be considered in isolation; import substitution is one alternative which can be considered, but not necessarily the only one, where the most important consideration should be given to the industry's potential dynamic effect. Efficiency consideration may or may not be relevant: in its initial inauguration, efficiency may be disregarded, but this does not suggest that there should not be a constant guard against perpetually maintaining industries regardless of cost and for continuously striving toward the achievement of efficiency as time passes. Once industries are established, however, their liquidation would not only be economically costly, but would also affect various vested interests.

In determining the course of industrial development, there is, of course, the question of the ownership of the means of production. Many governments have fostered industrialization through creating state enterprises because of ideological commitment, or merely because of the lack of private initiative, or for other reasons. Egypt, for example, has pursued socialist policy; foreign and domestic industrial enterprises were nationalized and new investments were concentrated in the government sector. India has proclaimed socialism but without nationalizing private industrial enterprises and reserving the development of new manufacturing fields to government. At one time or another, socialism has also been proclaimed and adhered to in Burma, Ceylon, Chile, Guinea, Indonesia, and Tanzania. Others leave it to private enterprise initiative, but even when there is no explicit commitment to socialist ideology, the role of public investment can still be relatively large, for example, in Brazil, Mexico, Pakistan, Taiwan, and Turkey. In Taiwan, shares of government enterprises were distributed as compensation for land reforms; in Mexico, government direct ownership was acquired through nationalization of foreign-owned enterprises, but in addition there are also joint ventures with local or foreign interests.

There is a possibility for symbiosis between private and public sectors (Brazil, Mexico). Persistent encouragement of the private sector, or a sympathetic attitude toward it, does not preclude the government from its role in influencing the course of industrialization, nor does it prevent the government from prodding the private sector through exercising its leverage. Mexico, for example, seemed to be able to apply a flexible policy because of the government power: while imposing direct controls on prices in the domestic market to facilitate industrialization, prices were occasionally forced down through the threats of tariff reduction and abolishment of import controls.[10]

In a mixed system, too much reliance on direct control could considerably tax and strain the government's administrative apparatus and possibly it would perform less favorably compared to fully fledged state control. (One could, for example, compare India and the People's Republic of China.) M. Haq has observed that "once direct controls were established, they breed like mushrooms .... And as the direct controls started replacing the market, the pyramid kept on building, till the government officials sitting on top of that did not know any longer what on earth they were controlling."[11] In comparison to India, Mason has suggested that "controls were less effective in Pakistan with the result that markets, black, gray and off-white, intruded more effectively than in India to redress some of the more distorting effects of controls."[12] Bhagwati and Desai have come to the opinion that "Indian economic policies in the industrial sector degenerated into an extravagant display of bureaucratic controls and restrictions, with these means turning into de facto ends."[13]

To summarize, it appears that the justification for industrialization lies in its becoming a potentially more powerful thrust to generate accelerated growth as compared to agriculture. With regard to a specific case, however, the realization of the potential will depend on the initial conditions of a particular country and since the strategy and policy for economic development would have to be viewed within an overall context, the dynamic potential of industrialization does not give sufficient ground for industries to be given priority over agriculture: at some level of development, there may be areas in agriculture which are potentially more dynamic than certain manufacturing industries. Nor does it provide justification for industrialization to put the emphasis on import substitution. The nature and composition of manufacturing industries is very important: their depth, as measured by the extent to which the industries are integrated to the national economy, is more important than their breadth, as measured by the number of factories located in the country.

The Development Center of OECD has published six volumes of country studies, dealing with the problems, processes, and policies of industrialization and trade in the developing countries of Brazil, India, Mexico, Pakistan, the Philippines, and Taiwan, and one comparative volume assessing the general industrialization and trade policies in these countries and Argentina.[14] The general observation seems to constitute an indictment of industrialization and trade policies in these countries, which have inefficiently and excessively encouraged import substitution; thus, the foreword by the president of the Center suggests that the studies "indicate that these countries have now reached the stage where policies that are followed to promote import-substitution are proving to be harmful for the economic development of these countries."[15]

Import Substitution and the
Cost of Industrialization

Given the technological inferiority of the developing countries, it is to be expected that import substitution (or any industrialization program) will distort the static efficiency criteria in the allocation of resources and that it will bring forth high-cost incipient manufacturing industries. However, despite the high initial costs, the justification for import substitution (or any industrialization program) is to be found in its potential dynamism, regardless of its efficiency as viewed in terms of the current structure of prices. Efficient incipient manufacturing industries are desirable, but are only of little avail, without the realization of their potential dynamism.

The OECD country studies, and the comparative volume, seems to suggest that policies which have been followed in those countries studied have not shown signs of decisive dynamic impacts in terms of growth in the overall economy, which would offset their high-cost and efficiency-distorting effects. In fact, it has been boldly proclaimed with regard to India that "the 'cut-off-imports-and-industrialize' strategy . . . neglects the very meaning of planning and leads to an indiscriminate growth of industries regardless of costs. . . . The nature and results of Indian experience . . . ought to disabuse economists and policy-makers of the attractiveness of such simplistic solutions. . . ."[16] If not negative, the dynamic impact of India's industrialization policies seems to have been considered minimal.

On the other hand, other countries seem to have indicated some positive roles for their industrialization policies; it must be emphasized, however, that in Mexico, Pakistan, and Taiwan, there have also been agricultural expansions. With regard to Mexico, it has been suggested that "by any standards, Mexican economic performance has been very impressive," although "in much of this success, Mexico has frankly been lucky"; in addition to its agricultural expansion, the government has given encouragement to the private sector and there has been relatively not much foreign exchange constraint.[17]

In Brazil, industrialization has been considered to have made a major contribution to significant modernization and to the growth of per capita income; it has been suggested that "the most important reasons for intervention to promote industry are based on dynamic considerations, and involve sacrificing maximum allocative efficiency now in order to shift to a structure of production which will permit increased income later."[18] Again, in Brazil the government "worked intimately" with the private sector and has shown "flexibility."

In Pakistan, industrialization policies have brought phenomenal growth of the modern industrial sector, although the comparative volume has suggested that the gain was substantially offset by the additional costs borne in other sectors; in any case, while in the 1950s per capita income failed to increase, a shift in policy during the

1960s "away from the strict rigidities" brought the growth in per capita income to greater than 2.5 percent.[19] In the Philippines, there were growth effects of the initial import substitution phase throughout the early 1950s although subsequently the domestic market was exhausted and the policy failed to maintain industrial growth. In Taiwan, the sequence of industrialization policies characterized by the declining importance of restrictive policies has been taken to play a role in its striking growth performance. Although in general Taiwan has guided the development of private industries through industrial licensing, controls have managed "to enlist private initiative instead of stifling it."[20]

The role of industrialization through import substitution policies has increasingly been questioned. On the whole, the volumes have made an attempt to study empirically the nature of import substitution in industry and its consequent costs to the economies, through the use of analytical techniques which facilitate estimation of the effective rates of protection, and through an examination of the impact of direct control which seems to have been considered as excessively encouraging import-substituting manufacturing industries at the expense of agriculture and exports. The volumes seem to have indicated that in countries where controls are less rigid (i.e., where private initiatives have been given more importance through more liberal, market-oriented policies), they are less prone to costly industrialization. Thus, the main thrust of the volumes does not appear to be an attack on the logic of industrialization through import substitution, but rather it is an indictment of the particular policies pursued which have not produced efficient results.

Consequently, there have emerged prescriptive policy measures for more efficient industrial development, focused on mitigating its excessive costs. While the comparative volume has recognized that "there may be some reason for favoring industry," alternative industrialization policies which would yield less defects than these manifested in the past might "lead, in the long run, to faster and most satisfactory growth."[21] Basically, the prescriptive measures are greater reliance on the price mechanism of the market and abandonment or decreased use of direct controls; lower and more uniform tariffs, and minimal quantitative import restrictions; more flexible and realistic exchange rates; encouragement of exports.[22] However, since industrialization through import substitution could easily produce a convenient framework for persistent high-cost industries, it is "unlikely to be in [the developing countries'] long-term interest."[23]

The argument, of course, hinges upon the question of the validity of the estimates for the excessive costs of industrialization through import substitution. Estimates for the effective rates of protection give rise to issues involving their conceptual and empirical hurdles; but even if the estimates are valid on both counts, it is not convincing to suggest that there is a causal relation between effective protection and emerging industrial structure (although among the countries studied Mexico and Taiwan have shown the lowest effective rates and domestic prices in these two countries for half or more of the manufactured goods examined were below world market prices plus tariffs). Furthermore, there is no easy way of measuring the impact of direct controls, as such, on efficiency, since direct controls have complex repercussions which would be difficult to quantify.

In any event, even if the estimates are accurate, excessive rates of protection and/or direct controls could merely be symptoms of inefficiency, and the fact that either one is correlated with inefficiency, by no means indicates causal relationship. In other words, it is conceivable that since import substitution tends to disregard the composition of industries thus being encouraged, inefficiency may be observed simply because the industries studied are in fact perpetually inefficient. For instance, industries being established may not correspond to the internal needs of the economy: excessive rates of protection and direct controls could be inherent in such industries which could not produce, to say nothing of maintaining, their own momentum. In this instance, excessive rates of protection and direct controls might be viewed as the consequences, rather than the causes, of inefficiency, arising from the wrong choice of industries. Mitigating, or undoing, the apparent defects of controls in the context of such a fundamental problem may be disastrous to the industry concerned, although not necessarily to the whole economy in the long run.

Thus it appears that unless the causal relationships between excessive rates of protection and direct controls on inefficiency are firmly established, more reliance on the market and liberalized policies could merely become another form of simplistic solution of a patchwork, plaster nature. In fact, there have been descriptions in these studies of periodic and partial attempts at a movement toward liberalization which was later abandoned: "it is significant that, despite the difficulties, these countries thought the attempt worth making."[24] It would seem that if excessive rates of protection and direct controls are inherent in an evolving but fragile industrial structure, the forces of the emerging vested interests would make reversal in liberalized policies inevitable.

In any case, there is a lesson to be learned from these OECD volumes of studies: industrialization through import substitution could create an evolving industrial structure with persistently high-costs manufacturing industries. Industrialization through import substitution is no longer an article of faith, but it gives rise to issues subject to disputes. Direct controls and quantitative restrictions, tariffs, multiple exchange rates, etc., have created a protected domestic market for manufacturing products, increasing the general level of prices while at the same time there exist no automatic corrective devices, contributing to policies which would discourage manufacturing as well as agricultural exports and lead to pressures on the balance of payments, leading to more controls, etc.[25] It constitutes a vicious circle, except that the consequent imbalances might produce unforeseen effects giving rise to the need for greater and greater controls and thence the circle spinning larger and larger.

Controls and the protected market impede the forces for domestic competition, producing a monopolistic or oligopolistic industrial structure. Although industrial capacity expanded and continued to become underutilized, there was a tendency for domestic prices to remain high.[26] Supportive measures for the new industrial ventures do not necessarily yield an increase in the employment opportunities which correspond to expanded capacity: favorable exchange rates for importing capital goods and lower rates of interest for their financing encourage the adoption of capital-intensive technique. Priority for the new import-substituting industrial ventures could subject the older lines of manufacturing activities and traditional handicrafts to increasing difficulties and they might even be displaced. The total effect might be the substitution of imported capital goods for local labor, lowering total employment and increasing import dependence. Consequently, existing inequality in the distribution of income might be aggravated.

Apart from its social implications and other factors, the consequent increasing inequality in the distribution of income might not even be justified on purely economic grounds. The monopolistic or oligopolistic profits of the new emerging class of industrialists may take the form of the difference between revenues and costs of production only in the accounting, but not in the economic, sense: the maintenance of its high rate is made possible only because the industrialists have gained special licensing and authorizations, privileges, and favors. Even in the face of excess capacities, profits may be gained by pressure on the government rather than through cost-cutting: the new class of industrialists might have "a 'proprietary' concept of production, far more than a spirit of enterprise in the true sense. . . . Experience shows how difficult and protracted it is, once this habit is established, to modify industrial structures or to change the outlook of producers."[27]

The heavy reliance of such monopolistic or oligopolistic profits on government policies may give birth to the new class of influence peddlers, their role becoming more important as the economy is enmeshed in a maze of administrative controls and as the administrative apparatus becomes more corrupt, inept, and cumbersome. Alliance between industrialists, influence peddlers, and government officials could consolidate their power and forge an elite whose sole concern is to become the perpetual guardian of their own interests and privileges. The high costs of industrialization, with its burden borne very unevenly by the different classes of society but more likely to be shouldered by the agricultural sector and the workers, are indeed a mere subsidy to the emerging elite of industrialists (indigenous and foreign) and their affiliates.

The emergence of such an elite group does not necessarily increase aggregate savings. Deteriorating terms of trade between agriculture and the nonagricultural sector, penalizing the former, could reduce its purchasing power and effective demand. Raising the general level of prices could reduce purchasing power and demand of the nonagricultural subsector not associated with the activities of the new industrial ventures. The shift in the distribution of income favoring the elite will shift demand, more to industrial goods but not necessarily those being produced domestically. The total effect may reduce aggregate demand for consumption goods produced domestically but not necessarily increasing domestic savings due to the linkages abroad.

If traditional exports decline because of rising domestic prices, manufacturing exports because their prices are out of line with world market prices, imported inputs increase to support the new industrial ventures, imported goods increase to satisfy the appetite of a wealthy emerging elite, total demand for domestically produced goods declines, government revenues decrease, and investible surpluses decrease and are misallocated, then all these factors will constitute formidable forces which will cause a country to move away from greater self-reliance and economic independence. The economy will instead become externally more dependent and vulnerable. In the industrialization process, efficiency consideration may be abandoned in the short run, but its disregard cannot be abused since the developing countries can least afford waste in the allocation of resources. The danger of import substitution lies in the possibility of industrialization catering only to the needs of a small high-income minority group, ignoring the backbone of the economy, when the country produces industrial goods which cannot generate a momentum, but instead strangle the economy with imminent crises.[28]

Agriculture

Many developing countries are thought to be predominantly agricultural; accordingly a great deal of writing has dealt with the role of agriculture in economic development. Thus, for example, it can be argued that agriculture could provide capital to the nonagricultural sector while the expansion of the latter would in turn stimulate demand for agriculture; given its backward state, the expansion of its production could be made possible by the introduction of new production methods.[29]

It has also been argued that the agricultural sector could contribute to economic growth and structural transformation through supplying a significant part of expanding labor needs and increased capital requirements from other sectors; fulfilling an expanded demand for food; being a source of demand for other sectors which is made effective through rising cash incomes in agriculture; and providing foreign exchange earnings for required imported inputs.[30] These can be collapsed into three forms of agricultural contribution to economic growth: *factor contribution* (transfer of productive inputs to other sectors), *product contribution* (increasing output), and *market contribution* (expanding intersectoral commercial relations, thereby raising the degree of monetization in the economy).[31]

Various cases have also been studied to lend support to the hypothesis that agriculture could contribute to structural transformation. It has commonly been maintained that in the United Kingdom the leading sector was cotton textiles and that agricultural revolution accompanied and preceded industrialization. It has also been suggested that one of the contributing factors for its industrialization was that up to 1830 its increasingly efficient agriculture was able to provide cheap food for most of the needs of its rapidly growing population.[32]

In Germany, in addition to the role of the state and banks in enhancing industrialization, iron and steel have been considered as the leading sectors, while in France railways have been regarded as providing the decisive impetus; on the other hand, it should be emphasized that before the onset of railways, there had been considerable improvements in French and German agriculture.[33] While in the United States, railways also played a crucial role, cotton exports have been considered as the main catalyst of its industrialization during the period 1820-40.[34] In the Soviet Union, an increase in agricultural productivity brought about through structural reorganization and mechanization freed a large number of workers for year-long off-the-farm work and it also transformed seasonal underemployment into seasonal unemployment and then mobilized it into productive use for capital formation.[35] In Japan exports of raw silk had facilitated the importation of capital goods for its industrialization until the domestic capacity was created.[36]

Johnston has analyzed and summarized Japanese agricultural development within the broader framework of the role of agriculture in economic development. It has been observed that the Japanese government applied the method of intensifying agriculture, thus increasing productivity, and from this, through heavy taxation, financed industry (at the same time the increase in production rendered possible the provision of relatively cheap food to the growing industrial workers).[37] Land tax was the main source of government tax receipts for about forty-five years. Introduced in 1873, it supplied some 86 percent of the central government's incomes throughout 1888-92, 80 percent in 1893-97, 63 percent in 1898-1902, and subsequently after the successful structural transformation declined to about 11 percent in 1933-37 (the ratio of direct taxes to income produced in agriculture averaged to 22 percent in 1883-87 and 16 percent in 1888-92).[38] Thus the high rate and the dominant weight of the land tax has been considered as a savings transfer out of agriculture, i.e., the initial establishment and the subsequent development of the modern sector depended on the accelerated growth of the traditional sector where the growing savings in agriculture were transformed into social overheads and factories.[39]

The case of Japan, the recent successes of agricultural growth in Mexico and Taiwan, and the high productivity of the new high-yielding varieties of seeds (rice, corn, wheat) have probably contributed to the high expectation placed upon the so-called Green Revolution.

If agricultural output can indeed be increased significantly without net resource transfer from other sectors (and instead, as is generally presumed with respect to the Japanese case, agriculture can add to the capital formation in the nonagricultural sector), then perhaps, as suggested by Maurice Dobb, it might be argued that the essence of the problem of structural transformation is not financial, but rather it is a question of economic organization (leaving aside its possible ideological overtone).[40] It has been commonly assumed that in the absence of foreign capital inflow, the limit of the possibility for industrialization, constituting a crucial bottleneck, is the availability of financial resources (savings) for large-scale investment. However, to speak of industrialization as being limited by the size of savings "only makes sense on the assumption that the margin between production and consumption can *only* be enlarged by lowering consumption and cannot be enlarged to any appreciable extent by enlarging total production. As soon as we dropped this assumption and allow the possibility of an increase in total production, the limit upon development of which we have spoken loses its absolute character, and may even cease to have much meaning as a limiting factor at all."[41] In the face of low productivity on the one hand, and the prospect for its improvement on the other, there is the possibility that agricultural improvement could yield product contribution, so that it could also enhance capital formation in the nonagricultural sector.

The discussions above might give the impression that the increase in agricultural productivity and its attending resource transfer is a prerequisite for industrial development. If one accepts the hypothesis that saving lies within the "vicious circle" of poverty (where saving is low because income is low, income is low because investment is low, and investment is low because saving is low), then an increase in agricultural productivity is a necessary means of breaking the circle.[42]

It has been remarked, however, that data assembled for several European countries for comparative studies have produced no conclusive evidence regarding the relative importance of the role played by surpluses derived from agriculture during the early phase of its industrialization (although in the later stages, many European aristocrats and other land receivers did invest considerable amounts in industry).[43] An increase in agricultural productivity, as such, may facilitate the emergence of additional surplus, but it does not necessarily ensure that such additional surplus would in fact be transformed into productive investment. In many developing countries, some surpluses derived from agriculture are simply used for lavish imported conspicuous consumption or are invested abroad.

On the other hand, the simple relation between savings and income as applied to individual developing countries is not in itself all that simple. Accordingly, a hypothesis suggesting that a country will need a higher income for achieving higher savings is not unquestionable. For example, Ethiopia and Tanzania are both listed as least developed, and both are predominantly agricultural; while gross agricultural production per economically active population in the former is slightly higher, the per capita GDP is lower, but only by 10 percent. Although economically the two countries are somewhat comparable, yet, while in 1960-62 the ratios of domestic savings to GDP in both countries are comparable (10.0 and 10.3 percent), by 1966-68 the savings rate declines in Ethiopia to 9.1 percent and it increases to 20.3 percent in Tanzania. This doubling of the savings rate in Tanzania could not be accounted for by the spectacular rise in its agricultural production since during 1960-69 per capita growth rates in agricultural production of the two countries were less than half a percentage point difference.

Thus, while an increase in agricultural production may facilitate higher savings, a higher level of savings may also be obtained without the concomitant increase in agricultural production. If the latter is true, the basic problem may lie in the way an economy is being organized; in fact, it may be argued further that if its organization is faulty, savings may remain low regardless of the increase in agricultural production.

Present Agriculture as Possible Source of Savings

In contrast to the relatively high rate of land tax for agricultural income in early Japan as noted above (greater than 15 percent before 1897), the rate in India during 1955-56 has been calculated as 1.9 percent.[44] While more than four-fifths of government revenues in Japan were from the agricultural sector prior to 1897, in the developing countries the highest ratio has been found to be less than one-third.[45]

A cursory look at the situation which exists in the

rural areas might lead to the impression that actually there might be a substantial realized surplus in the agricultural sector even at the present state of output condition. In the rural areas in Indonesia, the normal monthly rates of interest for cash advance from traditional money-lenders to the peasants range from 10 to 15 percent. Often, the peasants could not even obtain this type of credit, so they have to resort to buyer's credit on planted crops to be paid in kind during the harvest season (known as idjon), at an exorbitant profit to the buyer. Recently a Cabinet minister has suggested that the peasants merely obtain 20 percent of the value of their produce while the remainder accrues to the middlemen.[46] It may also be noted that the peasants also obtain the commodities not produced in the village through middlemen, who also extract high profits and usurious interest for credit advanced. In general, it appears that the individually weak peasants have to face a somewhat monopolistic market in the selling of this produce, and at the same time they also have to deal with a monopolistic market in the buying of their needs.

Egon Kemenes has studied in the African context the problem of agriculture as a possible source of savings.[47] It appears that the conditions found in Indonesia have also been observed in Africa as well, as the results of the research undertaken by various people and noted in his paper suggest. Thus in South Madagascar, according to Rudolff, interest paid for credit given for a few months is 40 percent or more; in some cases it is paid in kind and if calculated in money terms it may yield an annual rate of 75 percent; the limit value of 300 percent yearly may also be observed. Michele Saint Marc has observed that in some villages in Madagascar, advance money to be paid in kind merely camouflages a high interest rate while seed advance, given in kind, may yield an interest rate of between 50 and 300 percent. René Dumont, on the other hand, has suggested that the peasants in Africa pay up to 360 percent interest for money borrowed. In West Africa, the profit rates for handling agricultural produce may range from 50 to 70 percent.

The fact that the peasants are able to pay the usurious rate and support the high profit margin indicates that as far as the peasants are concerned, they have produced output exceeding their current consumption. It may also be noted that often the peasants still have to pay rent to the landlords. Whether the incomes squeezed from the farmers by the landlords, middlemen, and money-lenders are commensurate with the productivities of their respective functions may be subject to debate. However, these incomes which accrued to them constitute the peasants' savings (in the standard definition as the excess of current income over current consumption); if these incomes were wholly used up for consumption by them, the consolidation of accounts in the national income computation would eliminate the peasants' savings from the national picture. In this sense, the rate of savings has not much to do with the level of income, but rather it is being determined by the nature of economic organization. In fact, a higher agricultural production accompanied by greater capability to squeeze the peasants, the produce of whom is in turn utilized wholly for consumption, might decrease the aggregate rate of savings.

Since the agricultural sector is atomistic in nature and the group of landlords, traditional money-lenders, and middlemen is innumerable, the replacement of their function in order to ensure that the peasants' savings are the country's investment as well poses difficult organizational problems. Given the framework of political power structure, it does not seem that the problem can be discussed in generalized terms. While the world is tolerant of the existing situation, similar function of the landlords, middlemen, and money-lenders to be performed by the state (even if it would lead to higher investment) would sound the alarm for democracy and create indignant moral outcries for the suppression of human freedom and the emergent state's exploitation.

The Green Revolution

A cursory look at the trade pattern of some countries shows an anomaly: the industrially advanced countries with less population dependent on agriculture are major exporters of food, while the predominantly agricultural developing countries have utilized a substantial portion of their foreign exchange earnings for food imports. In Australia, Canada, and the United States, the ratios of those dependent on agriculture to the total population range from 8 to 12 percent, while in India the figures are probably in the range of 70 to 80 percent.[48] On the other hand, exports of cereals alone among agricultural commodities (the years chosen are arbitrary) account for about 18 percent of the total exports of Australia (1967), 12 percent in Canada (1968), and 11 percent in the United States (1966), while imports of cereals alone amount to about 20 percent of the total import bill in India (1966, mostly wheat) and imports of rice alone in Indonesia account for about 19 percent (1965).[49]

The developing countries of Africa probably spend more than 10 percent of their foreign exchange earnings for imports of foodstuffs. In the period 1960-68 gross food production in the developing countries grew at the rate of 2.6 percent annually according to both FAO and USDA figures, barely having kept up with the rate of population growth. Per capita food production grows less in the developing than in the developed countries. From a sample of 37 developing countries based on 1962-68 data, it has been found that 15 among them (including India, Pakistan, and Sudan) have become more dependent on imported foodstuffs; Taiwan and Mexico are among those with decreasing dependence.[50]

Agricultural aid from the developed to the developing countries, such as the United States PL 480, has generated mixed opinion regarding its effect on domestic agriculture. On the one hand, it has been argued in the case of India that it made possible the pursuit of a policy which

**FOOD PRODUCTION: PER CAPITA INDICES AND GROWTH
RATES IN DEVELOPING AND DEVELOPED COUNTRIES**
(Indices 1952-56 = 100)

Market economies	Per capita food production indices		Average annual rate of increase in gross food production index, 1962-68, in percent	
	1960	1968	FAO	USDA
Developed	111	127	3.0	2.2
Developing	105	107	2.6	2.6
Africa	104	99	2.8	1.5
Other Asia	108	110	3.0	2.4
West Asia	105	110		
Western Hemisphere	100	101	3.0	3.8

Sources: Review of International Trade and Development, 1970, World Economic Survey, 1969-1970.

thwarted agricultural development: in the face of inflationary pressures, imports through PL 480 permitted the holding of the price of wheat at an artificially low level, resulting in the deterioration of the terms of trade which penalized the farmers while favoring consumers in the urban areas, particularly the middle and high income groups.[51] Similar conclusions have been suggested with respect to Pakistan,[52] although it has been observed that "P.L. 480 shipments *may* have had an adverse impact on agricultural output in the 1950s but their availability in the 1960s made possible a number of measures which taken together with other actions bearing on farm incentives set the stage for a very substantial increase in agricultural productivity."[53]

On the other hand, compared to other countries, Israel obtained more United States agricultural aid per capita. It has been suggested, however, that the aid merely displaced imports from other countries, but did not impair domestic producers: the aid permitted the government to guarantee low and stable cereal prices to poultry farmers and with the importation of coarse grains utilized as feedstuffs in the poultry industry, Israel became an exporter rather than an importer of eggs.[54]

Whether agricultural aid is harmful or beneficial to the domestic agricultural development will probably depend on what the governments choose to do with it. As long as agricultural productivity remains low, the options opened to the governments are rather limited. Rising food prices directly affect the urban dwellers, who, after all, wield considerable political and economic power disproportionate to their sheer number as compared to the rural inhabitants. But agricultural aid is a mere palliative; its rise and fall fluctuates with the tide of international relations and is not very reliable. The basic problem lies in the low level of agricultural productivity, so that the need for agricultural aid should be examined within the context of its overall effect on domestic agricultural productivity, rather than from the narrower angle of its being able to temporarily redress a crisis.

The following table illustrates that although India has about eighty-five times as much manpower available per hectare as compared to the United States, yields per hectare are considerably lower for all of the following crops:

INDIA AND USA: YIELDS FOR MAJOR FOOD CROPS, 1964-65

(KG PER HECTARE)

Crops	India	USA
Wheat	730	1770
Maize	990	3930
Rice	1610	4590
Sorghum and millet	990	2580
Potatoes	8300	20700
Sweet potatoes and yams	6400	9400

Source: Maddison, Economic Progress and Policy in Developing Countries, p. 137.

The discrepancies might be due to differences in the use of fertilizers and chemicals, agricultural implements, and inferior seeds.

Although it has been presumed that the yields per hectare of rice and other crops during the Meiji Restoration were little if at all higher than those prevailing in the contemporary developing countries in Asia[55], Ishikawa has maintained that such is not the case, due to "misunderstanding" which "seems to have stemmed simply from an incorrect conversion of the Japanese measure (in terms of capacity in brown rice) into the measure adopted in most Asian countries (in terms of weight in paddy)."[56] His figures show that during the Meiji Restoration Japan had already attained a paddy yield of 2.3 metric tons per hectare, considerably higher than the yields in most of South and Southeast Asia, which were in the neighborhood of 1.3 metric tons (average figures for 1955-56 through 1960-61).[57]

Given the differences in productivities, there seems to be considerable scope for their increase through technological change. The United Nations ECAFE, for example, has urged the application of the "Japanese method of rice cultivation" to the developing countries of Asia.[58] In some ways, there are some similarities between the conditions which obtained in Japan during the Meiji era and those to be found in the contemporary developing countries.

Thus it may be noted that per capita income in Japan during the early Meiji era converted at the postwar rate of exchange was roughly $65 (higher at current prices).[59] Japan was also predominantly agricultural: the contribution of agriculture to national income was in the range of 63-68 percent; the percentage of population employed in agriculture was between 76-82 percent; and the proportion of rural to total population was about 80 percent.[60] Resource endowments were characterized by the scarcity of land and capital, on the one hand, and abundance of labor, on the other. The agrarian structure was of the form where the small peasants were dominant while the technical level adopted was not very sophisticated, where land was cultivated by manpower with simple agricultural implements.

There are, however, problems to be considered if one were to draw from the apparent similar inferences regarding the prospect of rapid growth in agriculture through technological change. In assessing this prospect, Ishikawa[61] has considered, among other things, two factors: the technical and the economic aspects. The following is largely based on his findings in examining the possibility of technological change in agriculture, as they are related to the conditions which exist in contemporary South and Southeast Asia (with due comparison to the conditions in Japan during the Meiji era).

Technical Aspect

While it is true that the new varieties have remarkable yield-increasing potential, shorter-period maturing property (opening up the possibilities for multiple cropping), and accordingly offer the prospect for high profitability, they at the same time require modern complementary inputs. These inputs as applied to the developing countries may represent a technically discontinuous jump from the traditional methods; in any case, the new varieties are technical borrowing in the most direct form, jumping from the traditional varietal improvements from the domestic stocks (lacking a distinct phase of pure-line selection as occurred in Japan and Taiwan).

The new varieties are fertilizer-responsive and their high productivity could be realized only if the crucial requirements pertaining to the quantity and quality of the complementary inputs are fulfilled. These are related to flood control, irrigation, and drainage facilities; modern agricultural machineries and implements; fertilizers and agricultural chemicals; and skilled labor.

A high standard of technical quality in irrigation and drainage facilities is essential to insure adequate water at specific intervals. On the other hand, the traditional gravity method does not permit the realization of the yield-increasing potential. By contrast, during the Meiji era, basically irrigation and drainage facilities had already been as high as at present and later projects were a mere improvement which did not present a fundamental change.

The introduction of multiple cropping requires timeliness: harvesting and threshing of the first crop must be undertaken almost simultaneously with land-tilling and transplanting of the second crop. This results in an increase in peak labor load, which, if it cannot be met, might require modern agricultural machineries and implements (tractors, power tillers, power threshers). In any case, the modern machineries and implements might be needed to ensure precision in farm operation. Regarding the state of labor instruments and power currently in use, Ishikawa has argued that modern machineries and implements also represent a discrete technical jump. In Japan, on the other hand, a fairly wide range of farm mechanization was reached only after passing through an intermediate stage which lasted from the Meiji era to the 1950s.

So far it has not been ascertained whether the great amount of fertilizer requirements should be met solely in the form of chemicals or whether it can be substituted by organic fertilizer, especially farm-yard manure. Chemical fertilizers have been the most important complementary input, but its utilization might yield negative results by altering the ecological environment, creating conditions suitable for the growth of a whole range of pests and insects; on the other hand, their elimination through the use of pesticides and insecticides may further create ecological problems. In any case, the production and uses of fertilizers in the developing countries are still in general low.

Thus, in contrast to the technical requirements, the state of modern inputs currently in use in South and Southeast Asia is not in general very adequate: irrigation facilities are not well fitted for the new varieties; the usage of farm machinery and agricultural implements is still rather meager; and the utilization of chemical fertilizers is still low. On the other hand, the technical requirements are interdependent. Thus the high-yielding potential can be realized only with substantial fertilizers and plant nutrients, which in turn necessitate guaranteed supplies of water at specified intervals. Without such a guarantee, there is the possibility that the yield will instead be lower than the use of the old varieties without these complementary inputs.

Even if the conditions could be improved in the near future, and all these requirements are readily available, their efficient utilization would require a high degree of skills which may not be able to be met immediately by the traditional farming units. In conclusion, the application of the new varieties seems to need a well coordinated and integrated plan, not to mention the attendant financial costs.

The Japanese experience in agricultural development since the Meiji era has generally been considered useful for the contemporary developing countries. This is due to the observed phenomenon that the intensive farming technique, i.e., raising farm productivity through an increase in current inputs (fertilizers, improved seeds, and better farming technique), adopted since the Meiji era, was apparently effective in increasing agricultural output. The relatively minor capital requirements for basic investments in irrigation have carried the impression that the rise in output was wholly attributable to the intensive farming technique.

What has commonly been ignored is the fact that basic investments had been undertaken extensively during the earlier Tokugawa era, which had made possible the attainment of a per hectare paddy yield of 2.3 metric tons in the subsequent Meiji Restoration. Thus it has been observed that "if we derive a lesson from the Japanese experience that the increase in land productivity can be attained solely by fertilizers, improved seeds and better farming techniques, this is irrelevant to the contemporary developing countries in South and Southeast Asia, except in specific areas where the basic investments have already been completed."[62]

Economic Aspect

The previous discussion purports to show that technically, the realization of the high-yielding potential of the new varieties would require inputs which, if to be compared to the state of their utilization in the developing countries (of South and Southeast Asia), might represent a sudden leap from what traditionally have been employed. The new varieties could facilitate easier adaptation of the lessons derived from the Japanese experience; however, if the experience drawn does not take into account the basic investments during the Tokugawa era, its costs to the developing countries may be grossly underestimated. The economic aspect of the problem is to relate fulfillment of the input requirements of the new varieties to the resource endowments which exist in the developing countries.

In contrast to the nonagricultural sector, the magnitude of working capital requirements in agriculture is relatively small. The main forms of capital are flood control, irrigation and drainage facilities, agricultural machineries and implements, and draft animals.

Compared to the situation in early Japan, the ratios of arable land to agricultural labor force as well as draft animals to agricultural labor are probably greater in the developing countries of South and Southeast Asia now. On the other hand, agricultural implements per farm household seem to be higher in Japan. There seems to be no definite evidence to indicate that the overall resource endowments per worker in agriculture are more favorable in Japan than in these developing countries. What is important to note is that while in the Japanese experience factor proportions utilized in production were in line with the resource endowments, in the developing countries they may diverge.

The high-productivity and yield-increasing new varieties have a land-saving effect, but the extent to which labor is substituting for land is yet unclear (except in the case of the introduction of multiple cropping). What is clear is that the role of capital is crucial in bringing about the desired effect so that instead of labor substituting for land, the new varieties are characterized more by the effect of capital substituting for land. Besides, capital also tends to substitute labor. The net effect is that the new varieties will tend to alter factor proportions utilized in production such that it may not be consistent with the available resource endowments.

Thus, for example, instead of the traditional water buffalo and disc plow (costing less than $150 per unit), which requires more unskilled labor, the use of a power tiller, small tractor, and disc plow drawn by a tractor requiring less (though more skilled) labor, may cost between $3,000 to $7,000 per unit. The former forms of capital are available locally while the latter in general have to be imported. An economic problem which arises is whether it will be warranted to introduce the new varieties, the full realization of which tends to displace local labor and draft animals in favor of modern agricultural implements with high import content. Furthermore, the increased use of chemical fertilizers, insecticides, and pesticides will certainly not raise the utilization of local resources in many developing countries, but rather it will also increase the import bill.

By contrast, the land-saving effect was partly achieved through an increase in Japanese labor input and partly through increased capital inputs but which had been constructed and manufactured in a highly labor-intensive manner in Japan, and not imported. The contrast is significant because while in the Japanese experience the land-saving technique was also labor-using, the adoption of the new varieties in the developing countries might produce both land-saving and labor-saving effects. In addition to greater imported agricultural inputs, it might aggravate rural unemployment as well.

In addition, as has been emphasized earlier, intensive farming technique requires guaranteed supplies of water, without which the complementary inputs might become infructuous or even make the new varieties yield less than the old without these inputs. It may be noted, however, that investment in irrigation is a high-cost undertaking, particularly if it involves fundamental changes in the system as apparently required by the new varieties. The huge investment required and the returns to be expected often provide the ground for criticisms from a purely efficiency consideration. The Seyhan project in Turkey has been considered a heavy burden on the economy while the Galoya project in Ceylon cost $125 million. Water development projects and irrigation in Brazil and Pakistan have been criticized.[63] The Shihmen Dam and Reservoir cost $70 million, although Jacoby has suggested that its return has been only about 1.5 percent annually (in contrast to riskless long-term loans which could yield 12 percent or more).[64]

In short, the widespread adoption of the new varieties is a highly capital-intensive proposition which in many developing countries may involve high opportunity costs (in domestic money terms as well as in foreign exchange) and may also lead to the displacement of local resources (involving social cost). Government policies and foreign aid may facilitate reduction of the prices of imported inputs, but this may result in the relative profitability of substituting chemical fertilizers and agricultural machineries for domestic labor. Such policies, therefore, retard the efforts in utilizing as much as possible the locally made and locally available resources and they will create wider divergence between factor proportions adopted in production and the given domestic resource endowments.

Given the enormous potential for increased yield, the costs might be worth it. However, it is a subject which needs to be studied and scrutinized carefully, not merely from the standpoint of partial analysis (where there might be distortion in relative prices favoring the substitution of imported inputs for local resources, and where there might arise an inadequacy of calculating the economic costs alone), but rather from the perspective of the whole economy and its overall implications.

If all factors seem to point to the advisability of adopting the new varieties, the diffusion problem of the new technology for its widespread application should not be underestimated. The diffusion problem is probably more difficult than in industry and it may need well-developed extension services, demonstration projects, farmers associations and cooperatives, institutions which played a large role in the development of agriculture in Japan and Denmark. Besides, there will also be need for well-developed marketing network, transport, and storage facilities.

The high capital requirements of the new varieties could also be put in juxtaposition with the fact that the small peasants now barely live in subsistence level and are still in the state of perpetual debt. The greater financial requirements may lead them into deeper control and manipulation by the middlemen and the rural money-lenders. The new varieties may favor the big landowners who are in the position of reaping the benefits accrued from the economies of scale, of financing increased capital expenditure outlays, of exerting pressure for favorable exchange rate for imported inputs, of hiring skilled labor, etc. (where the process may create further income inequality within the agricultural sector, further increasing social cost).

Ishikawa has noted that in West Bengal, India, the response to the high-yielding variety was greater the larger the size of the farms; that in Central Luzon, the Philippines, there was a tendency for noncultivating and partly-cultivating landlords to become commercialized farmers. The Japanese experience, on the other hand, suggests that there are two phases: in the first, there had been bipolarization in the agrarian structure, where the weight of large-sized farmers increased after 1890, subsequently followed around 1920 by the concentration of agrarian structure to medium-sized farmers.

All this may point to the conclusion that without proper, well coordinated and integrated planning and a sense of perspective, it cannot be presumed that the Green Revolution, merely because it occurs in the agricultural sector, will necessarily be beneficial to the small peasants, and hence the masses of the developing countries. If all the costs are calculated, it is quite possible that in some countries, there will be a need for a large resource transfer to the agricultural sector rather than the other way around, at least in the initial stage where massive expenditures for infrastructure might be required. Without corrective measures, the position of the landlords, middlemen and rural money-lenders might become more dominant and better well-entrenched; in effect, such resource transfer from the nonagricultural sector is nothing more than a subsidy for the consolidation of their economic power. The exodus of the displaced rural labor force to the urban sector might further increase the social overhead costs.

If all the implications are considered, the Green Revolution might be short of a miracle. The following illustrative case seems to point out that to the small peasants, it is a far cry from a miracle. Much enthusiasm has been generated by the phenomenally high growth rate of agriculture in Mexico; some have suggested that the Mexican experience should become a model for other developing countries. On the other hand, Leopoldo Solis has observed that the majority of the owners of small plots live on a subsistence level and, besides, they are still in the hands of local money-lenders: accordingly, many of them have to look for work as migrant farm laborers in the United States, or as temporary laborers on large farms, or migrate to cities.[65]

Recent Experience: Mexico

In the postwar years only four countries have achieved high growth rates in agriculture among the developing countries, at an annual rate of almost 5 percent or more:

Israel, Mexico, Taiwan, and Venezuela. In Taiwan, during
the Japanese occupation, the share of irrigated land in
total area under cultivation increased considerably and the
country was made (through the use of police force in some
cases) familiar to the Japanese technique of intensive
cultivation as well as the high-yielding varieties: the foundation for increased agricultural productivity had accordingly been formed over a period of about four decades.[66] Israel and Taiwan have benefited from large
foreign aid.[67] Venezuela, on the other hand, has considerable financial resources to finance agricultural
improvement.

The case of Mexico has been emphasized by Schultz as
a lesson to the low-income countries seeking to develop a
modern economy through the transformation of the traditional agriculture; in his opinion, the case is especially
important since Mexico entered upon an unusually high
rate of growth in agricultural production very recently
while on the other hand the foundations for growth were
not laid down by an earlier gradual development spread
over many decades.[68] The rapid growth of agriculture was
achieved through land reform, research and application of
new, modern, and imported techniques, and the building
of an infrastructure (highways, dam, irrigation).

It might appear that agriculture has been a contributing factor in Mexico's high growth of GNP. According to
Leopoldo Solis, the postwar development of Mexico is
marked by two clearly distinct stages: the first stage is
from the end of the Second World War to 1956, which had
been an *outward-oriented growth*, characterized by inflation, subsequently followed by an *inward-oriented growth*
based on import-substitution and stable prices. In both
stages the growth rates of GNP at constant prices are 6.2
percent annually.

Until 1956, agriculture grew at an annual rate of 7.5
percent, higher than the growth in GNP, and there was a
considerable expansion in agricultural exports, offsetting
the decline in earnings due to the stagnation of mineral
exports. Subsequently there was a slowing down in invest-

ment of social overhead as well as in agricultural research and development, and the growth rate of agriculture then declined to less than 4 percent, lower than the GNP growth rate.

While the Porfirio Diaz regime distributed about 80 million hectares to, among others, big companies (by 1910, around 12 percent of the landed property belonged to the foreigners), Lazaro Cardenas began intensive distribution of land to the peasants (about 18 million hectares during 1934-40) through expropriation of the former *haciendas*, a policy which was followed by the subsequent presidents. There emerged than a system of *ejido*, where the expropriated land became communal ownership (the land belongs to the peasants who can toil it and bequeath it, but who can legally neither sell nor rent it), together with the peasants' ownership of small private plots (unaffected by the land reform).

Most observers seem to agree that the *ejido* is now in a state of crisis or stagnant.[69] On the other hand, the conditions of the small private plots are getting worse: "the majority of the owners of small plots live on a subsistence level. Like their *ejidatario* peers, they are characterized by low productivity and a limited technical level, besides which they are still in the hands of local money-lenders."[70] The commercialization of agricultural products also faces a somewhat similar situation as was mentioned with respect to Africa: "there are monopolistic conditions conducive to price-fixing that hamper the formation of capital in agricultural units. It is frequently pointed out that the middlemen make the largest profits, for they buy from small, unorganized farmers—to whom they have often lent money—and later sell as monopolist to the regional market."[71]

If the *ejido* and small private plots (*minifundio*) are characterized by low productivity (and low yield), what factors account for the high growth rate of agriculture in Mexico? The rapid growth rate is a fact, as was the considerable investment in dams, irrigation, and highways, which have allowed easy access to markets.

According to Flores de la Pena, noted in Solis' article, after thirty years of Agrarian Reform, Mexico is still a country of "large landholders" while the concentration of property is to be found particularly in the areas under irrigation. Stavenhagen has attributed the prevalent form of *neo-latifundia* (modern, commercial agriculture on large properties, of recent origin) to the way land was distributed in newly irrigated regions.[72] Pena and Porragas have observed that greater productivity obtained on larger properties and agricultural progress is more marked in the areas under irrigation.[73]

While the *ejidos* and private small plots have persisted in the state of impoverished condition, increases in agricultural output in recent years have occurred in the *neo-latifundia* growing cotton, beans, and wheat.[74] The growth has occurred in the North and Pacific North regions, which are sparsely populated, arid, and dry, and have been the greatest beneficiary of investment in irrigation.

The analysis of cotton and wheat yields in seven states on a state-by-state basis suggests that the bulk of the increase in production may have been accounted for by "expansion of irrigation into new areas of northern Mexico where techniques, machinery, fertilizers, insecticides and credit from the United States were adopted."[75] It may also be noted that the ceilings imposed on cotton acreage in the United States had made it more attractive to grow cotton in Mexico and consequently there was an access to considerable financial assistance.

Thus, in examining the case of Mexico, Raj has observed that past experience suggests that

> however high the resulting growth rates in agriculture might be over certain periods, such development does not necessarily lead to transformation of agriculture but often only to the emergence of dualism within this sector. That the Mexican experience during this period has nevertheless been cited as a demonstration of the possibility of transforming traditional agriculture is a

remarkable example of the kind of casual empiricism that is abundantly in evidence in the literature on development problems.[76]

The dualistic nature of Mexican agriculture is indicated by the distribution of income in this sector. According to Weisskoff's figures, in 1963, within the agricultural sector, 60 percent of the families received 26.4 percent of income while the top 5 percent obtained 25.8 percent. Solis has also noted the dual nature of Mexican agriculture: agriculture absorbs 50 percent of the labor force and contributes less than 20 percent of the value added in the production process; within agriculture, there is the modern sector which can compete internationally in terms of efficiency and productivity, generating 65 percent of agricultural output though merely employing 36 percent of the agricultural labor force; the traditional sector, on the other hand, continues to have a backward technology and a low productivity but employs the larger part of the agricultural labor force.

General Observation

The previous chapter underlined the nonhomogeneous nature of the developing countries, pointed out the divergent initial conditions existing among these countries as well as compared to the presently developed economies in their earlier stage of development, and observed the tendency for growth polarization favoring the richer and/or the more industrialized developing countries. The discussion in this chapter seems to point out that the factors generally considered as determining growth are not particularly favorable to the poorer and/or less industrialized developing countries, which, as may be recalled, are also populated by the majority in the growth of developing countries.

The poorer developing countries could be handicapped in their mobilization of domestic resources, setting a low

limit to investment while at the same time they might need
to invest in projects with high capital-coefficients, and do
not appear to be characterized by greater foreign capital
inflows. Even if they choose to attract foreign investment,
the option available seems to be restricted to a resource-
induced type of investment, and could later be victimized
by technological obsolescence. On the other hand, their
structure of underdevelopment limits the areas through
which they could reap the benefits of technical progress, a
primary force determining growth in the twentieth century. Since their handicaps are fundamental in nature,
foreign assistance might merely assume the role of patchwork plaster and too much reliance on it could lead to
growing underdevelopment, making the developing countries more and more externally dependent and vulnerable.

NOTES

1. In the case of Brazil, for example, it has been suggested that
   "foreign firms have made extensive use of used equipment
   which would otherwise have been scrapped as economically
   obsolete in their home-country plants. Such equipment available
   to the firm at an opportunity cost little higher than its scrap
   value may still have a useful economic life in the conditions of a
   less developed economy. For example, equipment that has been
   scrapped for machinery of greater capital-intensity or larger optimal scale may be economic because of different relative factor
   prices or a smaller market size." [N. H. Leff, *The Brazilian
   Capital Goods Industry, 1929-1964* (Cambridge: Harvard University Press, 1968), p. 26].
2. For some capital goods industries, the local firms appeared to be
   able to withstand competition: although throughout 1945-62
   most equipment entered Brazil without tariff or import restrictions, and sometimes under a preferential exchange rate, the
   Brazilian capital goods industries had supplied 61 percent of the
   domestic requirements by 1947-49 and 75 percent by 1965 (see
   ibid.).

3. Even if labor is abundant and its actual marginal product in agriculture is zero, those laborers who are maintained and supported by their relatives could still obtain a higher subsistence wage level approximately equal to the average product in agriculture through the sharing of poverty. These laborers, however, could not be attracted to the manufacturing sector at the existing wage, but rather should be induced by a higher wage. Since in this case the subsistence wage is already overvalued and exceeds the true social opportunity cost as determined by the marginal product in agriculture, it could be argued that manufacturers should be subsidized or protected for their paying the overvalued industrial wage. It is, however, not necessary for the argument to rest on the zero marginal product case in agriculture, as long as there is an observed considerable divergence between agricultural and industrial wages. (See W. A. Lewis, "Economic Development with Unlimited Supplies of Labor," *Manchester School of Economic and Social Studies,* May, 1954, and E. E. Hagen, "An Economic Justification for Protection," *Quarterly Journal of Economics,* 1958.)

4. J. Viner, *International Trade and Economic Development* (Oxford, 1953).

5. See *The Economy of Latin America and Its Principal Problems* (New York: United Nations, 1950). In the report for the first UNCTAD meeting, however, the dangers of excessive protection were stressed and greater emphasis on exports of manufactured goods was urged [see *Towards a New Trade Policy for Development,* Report by the Secretary General, UNCTAD, Document E/Conf. 46/3 (New York: United Nations, 1964)].

6. See H. G. Johnson, *U.S. Economic Policies towards the Less Developed Countries* (Washington: Brookings, 1966), and B. Balassa, "Tariff Protection in Industrial Countries," *Journal of Political Economy,* December, 1965. See also R. Soligo and J. J. Stern, "Tariff Protection, Import Substitution and Investment Efficiency," *Pakistan Development Review,* Summer, 1965.

7. G. Myrdal, *An International Economy* (London, 1956), p. 276.

8. A. O. Hirschman, *The Strategy of Economic Development* (New Haven: Yale University Press, 1958), p. 121.

9. J. M. Fleming, "External Economies and the Doctrine of Balanced Growth," *Economic Journal,* June, 1955.

10. Whenever local prices were manifestly and unjustifiably higher than the international prices [see R. Izquierdo, "Protectionism

in Mexico," in R. Vernon (ed.), *Public Policy and Private Enterprise in Mexico* (Cambridge: Harvard, 1964)].

11. M. Hag, *The Strategy of Economic Planning* (Karachi: Oxford University Press, 1966), p. 51.

12. E. S. Mason, *Economic Development in India and Pakistan* (Cambridge: Center for International Affairs, Harvard, 1966), p. 15.

13. Bhagwati and Desai, *India: Planning for Industrialization* (see note 14), pp. 7-8.

14. The series has been published for the Organisation for European Economic Co-operation and Development, Paris, by Oxford University Press, New York, 1970. For the comparative volume, see I. Little, T. Scitovsky, and M. Scott, *Industry and Trade in Some Developing Countries: A Comparative Study.* For the country studies, see J. Bergsman, *Brazil: Industrialization and Trade Policies*; J. N. Bhagwati and P. Desai, *India: Planning for Industrialization*; T. King, *Mexico: Industrialization and Trade Policies Since 1940*; S. R. Lewis, Jr., *Pakistan: Industrialization and Trade Policies*; J. H. Power and G. P. Sicat, *The Philippines: Industrialization and Trade Policies*; and Mo-Huan Hsing, *Taiwan: Industrialization and Trade Policies.* In the subsequent footnotes, the country studies will be referred to by the name of the corresponding country while the comparative volume by *Comparative.*

15. *Comparative,* foreword.

16. *India,* p. 500.

17. *Mexico,* pp. 150-151.

18. *Brazil,* p. 185.

19. *Pakistan; Comparative,* p. 73. It may be noted that national averages have obscured important regional differences in Pakistan: the rate of industrialization, as measured by the increase in the share of industrial output in GDP, has been much lower in East than West Pakistan; in fact, it has been argued that from the standpoint of the share of industrial employment in total labor force, throughout the decade between the two census years of 1951 and 1961, East Pakistan failed to industrialize while West Pakistan achieved a significant rate of industrialization (the percentage of the labor force employed in agriculture

increased from 84.7 to 85.3 in the East and decreased from 65.3 to 59.3 in the West). The differential rates of industrialization, accompanied by differential rates of growth of income, led to a widening disparity of per capita incomes in the two regions. While it has been argued that these rates of disparity would appear to understate the real differential between the regional standards of living, these figures are nevertheless suggestive: in 1949-50, per capita income in the West was 17 percent higher than that in East Pakistan; the difference increased to 32 percent by 1959-60 and to 60 percent by 1969-70. [See K. Griffin and A. R. Khan (eds.), *Growth and Inequality in Pakistan* (London: Macmillan, 1972), p. 3.]

It has been argued that such a situation was the direct consequence of the government's extraordinary determination and single-minded pursuit of a strategy which emphasized acceleration in the growth of GNP. Until recently, the strategy essentially contained two elements, viz., first, the expansion was to occur largely through industrialization, and secondly, it was to be financed partly by the redistribution of income favoring the capitalist class, presumed to have a high propensity to save, and partly by foreign aid. The quasi-autarchic industrialization strategy and its method of financing have produced results whereby first, "Pakistan has been neglecting agriculture relative to industry and has been producing the wrong industrial goods in the wrong way and, moreover, has been doing so inefficiently," and secondly, "The process of redistributing resources from agriculture to industry was accompanied by, and in fact was an integral part of, a redistribution of income from the poor to the rich and from East to West Pakistan." (*ibid.*, p. 26.)

20. *Taiwan*, p. 189.
21. *Comparative*, p. 114, p. 312.
22. *Comparative*, chaps. 7, 9, 10.
23. *Comparative*, p. 391.
24. *Comparative*, p. 389.
25. *Comparative*, pp. 158-265.
26. *Comparative*, pp. 83-100.
27. *Comparative*, foreword.
28. Regional cooperation in industry is a special case of regional economic cooperation and integration: underlying it is the postulate that industrialization acts as a potentially powerful propeller for accelerated development. Advanced and modern

technology to be adopted in many sectors within the manufacturing industries is characterized by the economies of scale: lowest unit cost to be obtained from adopting this kind of technology requires that production achieves a certain minimum level. Failure to meet this minimum requirement would lead to higher unit cost since the manufacturing plants could either be too small or too large (given the market size limitation, manufacturers may opt for many small plants with relatively backward technology or one modern plant with unutilized installed capacity). Thus, pessimistic conclusions regarding the developing countries have often been aired and the possibility for extending industrial development beyond the limits of national boundaries explored.

Applying the traditional theory of economic integration to the special case of regional cooperation in industry, there are static and dynamic gains which might be expected from cooperation. The former, in the form of a rising living standard and welfare realized through the freer movements of factors of production and outputs, could be analyzed through the standard theory of customs union: these gains will be the greater the higher the stage of integration [see J. E. Meade, *The Theory of Customs Union* (Amsterdam: North Holland Publishing Co., 1955)]. Dynamic gains, on the other hand, would be obtained through economies of scale (realized as a result of the scale of operation of an individual plant); external economies (as a consequence of an expansion in the industry or in the whole economy due to their respective intersectoral relationships, where the growth in each sector has favorable repercussions on others); improved productivity (by lifting trade restrictions, domestic industries are subjugated to competition from intraregional trade); and through the removal of risks and uncertainty [see T. Scitovsky, "Two Concepts of External Economies," *Journal of Political Economy*, April, 1954; B. Balassa, *The Theory of Economic Integration* (Homewood, Ill.: Irwin, 1961), and "A Theory of Economic Integration," in M. S. Wionczek (ed.), *Latin American Economic Integration* (New York: Praeger, 1966); H. B. Chenery, "Comparative Advantage and Development Policy," *(American Economic Review*, March, 1961).

Both the static and dynamic gains entail trade-creation and trade-diversion. The former is cost-saving, resulting from the shift from higher-cost to lower-cost producers within the grouping; it refers to an increase in intraregional trade, which, on the usual assumptions, increases the output of the whole region while leaving no member country worse-off. The latter, on the other hand, is cost-increasing since import-substitution entails higher production costs; it refers to the diversion of trade from the lower-cost producers in the rest of the world to higher-cost ones in the grouping due to common external tariffs, which, on the usual assumptions with unchanged terms of trade, reduces the income of the whole grouping.

It has been maintained, on the one hand, that regional grouping is desirable only if its consequent trade-creation is greater than the trade-diversion [J. Viner, *The Customs Union Issue* (New York: Carnegie Endowment for International Peace, 1950)]; on the other, it has been argued that trade-diversion is not bad in all cases (R. G. Lipsey, "The Theory of Customs Unions: Trade-diversion and Welfare," *Economica*, February, 1957). As applied to the developing countries, there could be efficient trade-diversion which enables these countries to impose restrictions on noninput imports from the developed countries while enjoying the benefits of free trade among themselves (S. B. Linder, "Customs Union and Economic Development," in *Latin American Economic Integration*). Besides, trade effects are not the only ones to be considered as the ultimate criterion boils down to what industrial cooperation does to accelerated industrialization and growth, if the consideration is to be limited to its economic aspect alone.

The crucial assumptions underlying the traditional theoretical framework are that in each country there exist behavioral patterns such that relative prices reflect real production rates of transformation. As will be elaborated in another chapter, facts probably depart more from these assumptions rather than their being in conformity: there are fundamental differences between the developed and the developing countries. Improved productivity brought about through subjugating domestic industries to competition could be experienced only if there existed a highly differentiated production structure already (to be found in the developed countries); thus, the case is not particularly relevant to some developing countries, and wholly irrelevant to those which are still at the nonindustrial stage. Many developing countries are not currently primarily faced with the problem of adjusting the allocation of the given resources more efficiently but rather with the problem of expanding the production possibility frontier and finding productive employment for increasing unutilized factors of production (particularly unemployed or underemployed labor).

From the three remaining arguments for industrial cooperation, it may be noted that the removal of risks and uncertainty could be achieved through other means of cooperation while external economies are directly related to the allocation of industries, so they presuppose the prior acceptance of the idea of industrial cooperation. Hence, the only relevant argument is based on the economies of scale, directly related to the size of the market, in conjunction with the corresponding choice of techniques. The relevance of economies of scale in the production method of simple basic necessities is subject to question; on the other hand, many nonindustrial-stage developing countries are even lacking in these types of industry. It is doubtful whether economies of scale are a relevant factor to be considered for these countries: there may still be some scope, and some wisdom, in adopting simpler and labor-intensive production techniques which are not subject to market limitation and can still be adequately supported by the size of the domestic market. The fact that these countries are still at a lower stage of industrialization might be due to the fundamental deficiencies (lack of basic skills, capital, resources, infrastructure, organizational, managerial, and technical talents, etc.), not necessarily due to market-size limitation. Premature industrial cooperation among countries with these basic deficiencies could only provide fertile ground for the takeover and control by foreign or multinational corporations, or at least greater dependence on foreign experts and foreign capital, at the expense of national consumers who have to pay higher prices.

There are problems related to the interpretation of economies of scale [see M. Clement, R. Pfister, and K. Rothwell, *Theoretical Issues in International Economics* (Boston: Houghton Mifflin, 1967)]. Even if there exist unequivocal economies of scale, it is still subject to dispute whether a large, more efficient plant in one locality is necessarily preferable to many smaller and less efficient plants dispersed in different locations, especially if these factors were to be taken into consideration: that in many developing countries, the main problem is more of activating unutilized production capacity and perhaps in balanced regional development within the national economy as well; that larger plant tends to be more capital-intensive, requiring imported capital equipment and less of local labor (while for the smaller ones domestically produced equipment may suffice); that transport costs may offset production cost-saving. If economies of scale do in fact exist, the implication is that monopoly rights should be issued to those industries established under the provision of regional cooperation and the benefits to be accrued to the region will depend on how the allocations of the monopoly industries are being made. The gain from cooperation to the region will be maximized if such industries were allocated to the most efficient countries and it will considerably be reduced if allocated to the least efficient: thus, maximization of regional benefit may lead to the polarization of industrial growth and it is likely that its pursuit will lead to its skewed distribution, favoring the more developed member countries (see D. M. Schydlowsky, "Allocating Integration Industries in the ANDEAN Group," *Journal of Common Market Studies*, January, 1971). Such polarization is most likely to be unacceptable to the less developed member countries, so that the distributional constraint in the allocation of industries will reduce the potential gain to the region.

Regional cooperation is merely a cooperation between countries in a given geographical confine and it does not ensure that the member countries are at similar level of development nor at the same stage of industrial development; on the other hand, differences in the stage of industrialization and the level of development affect cooperation schemes in a double-edged manner. First, the less developed member countries fear polarization of industrial development favoring the more developed: integration of countries with different stages of industrial development tends to stagnate the infant industries in the less developed members; even within a national boundary, economic growth has produced increasing intraregional divergence rather than moving toward convergence (see R. S. Bhambri, *Economia Internazionale*, May, 1962, and J. G. Williamson, "Regional Inequality in the Process of National Development: A Description of the Patterns," *Economic Development and Cultural Change*, vol. 13, 1965). In practice, the issue of unequal industrial growth at the expense of the less developed member countries has emerged in various regional groupings [see, for example, *Latin American Integration and International Co-operation*, Organization of American States, Advisory Office on Integration, UP/G.38/1, March 10, 1972; M. S. Wionczek, "The Rise and the Decline of Latin American Economic Integration," and "Status and Prospects of Economic Integration Movements in the Developing Countries," in M. S. Wionczek (ed.), *Economic Co-operation in Latin America, Africa and Asia; A Handbook of Documents* (Cambridge: MIT Press, 1969); H. Brewster, *Industrial Integration Systems*, UNCTAD document, TD/B/345, July 12, 1971; S. Fagan, *Central American Economic Integration*, Research Series No. 15, Institute of International Studies, Berkeley, 1970; D. E. Ramsett, *Regional Industrial Development in Central America* (New York: Praeger, 1969); A. Hazelwood, *African Integration and Disintegration* (London: Oxford University Press, 1967)].

Secondly, on the other hand, the more developed member countries could fear structural readjustment due to competition from labor-cheap less developed members, as exemplified by the case of Venezuela with respect to ANDEAN, of Costa Rica to CACM, and Jamaica with respect to CARIFTA [described respectively in Wionczek, "The Rise and the Decline of Latin American Economic Integration"; A. Inotai, "The Central American Common Market," *Studies on Developing Countries*, Budapest, 1971, and El-Staley, "Costa Rica and the Central American Common Market," *Economia Internationale*, no. 1, 1962; *Regional Co-operation in Industry* (United Nations publication, Sales No. E.69.II.B.39), vol. 18, and *Commercio Exterior*, November, 1968)].

Thus, for both the less developed and the more developed member countries, the benefits from industrial integration are not immediately evident. The costs, on the other hand, are immediately felt, particularly by the less developed member countries: the tariff revenues foregone; the difference between the world and regional market prices of the commodities produced in the region (the burden is proportional to the amount of consumption in the corresponding member countries); the structural readjustment as the result of cooperation. The burden of industrial cooperation will be increasingly felt if there are persistent deficits in the intraregional trade balances of some member countries. Regional cooperation in industry is a short-term proposition, but these factors could create crises in the short run. There has been a tendency to think that the problem could be redressed if only there exists a mechanism for ensuring the equitable distribution of the costs and benefits of regional cooperation in industry; such a mechanism is difficult to apply and in the final analysis, evaluation of the costs and benefits of integration may have to be qualitative in nature and will rest on the exercise of judgment (see P. Robson, *Fiscal Compensation as a Means of Contributing to an Equitable Distribution of the Costs and Benefits Associated with Economic Groupings among Developing Countries*, UNCTAD document, TD/B/322, July 31, 1970). Even if such a mechanism could be found, it will be likely to be unsatisfactory as long as it is merely in the form of a financial transfer which does not fulfill the basic objective of industrial cooperation, viz., the structural transformation of all the individual member countries.

29. See W. A. Lewis, *The Theory of Economic Growth* (London: Allen and Unwin, 1955).
30. See B. F. Johnston and J. W. Mellor, "The Role of Agriculture in Economic Development," *American Economic Review*, September, 1961.
31. See S. Kuznets, "Economic Growth and the Contribution of Agriculture," in C. Eicher and L. Witt (eds.), *Agriculture in Economic Development* (New York: McGraw-Hill, 1964).
32. W. H. Nicholls, "The Place of Agriculture in Economic Development," (*ibid.*).
33. J. H. Clapham, *The Economic Development of France and Germany, 1815-1914* (Cambridge, Cambridge University Press, 1928).
34. D. North, *The Economic Growth of the United States: 1790-1860* (Englewood Cliffs: Prentice-Hall, 1961).
35. C. K. Wilber, *The Soviet Model and Underdeveloped Countries* (Chapel Hill: University of North Carolina Press, 1969). Also A. Erlich, "Preobrazhenski and the Economics of Soviet Industrialization," *Quarterly Journal of Economics*, February, 1950.
36. W. W. Lockwood, *The Economic Development of Japan: Growth and Structural Change, 1868-1938* (Princeton, Princeton University Press, 1954).
37. B. F. Johnston, "Agricultural Productivity and Economic Development in Japan," *Journal of Political Economy*, December, 1951.

38. K. Ohkawa and H. Rosovsky, "The Role of Agriculture in Modern Japanese Economic Development," in Eicher and Witt (eds.), *op. cit.*
39. K. Ohkawa and H. Rosovsky, "A Century of Japanese Economic Growth," in W. W. Lockwood (ed.), *The State and Economic Enterprise in Japan* (Princeton, Princeton University Press, 1965).
40. M. Dobb, "Some Problems of Industrialization in Agricultural Countries," in *Some Aspects of Economic Development; Three Lectures.*
41. *Ibid.*, p. 37. Delhi School of Economics, Occasional Papers, No. 3, 1951.
42. R. Nurkse, *Problems of Capital Formation in Underdeveloped Countries* (Oxford: Basil Blackwell, 1955). There appears to be two aspects in Nurkse's model: the supply and the demand aspects. On the supply side it has been assumed that there exists surplus labor in the agricultural sector (with zero marginal productivity) the consequence of which is that labor can be withdrawn from this sector while maintaining agricultural output constant (i.e., it is possible to increase output per unit of labor by simply withdrawing the surplus manpower). On the other hand, the transfer of labor does not involve an increase in the demand for agricultural product such that it could not be met by the output of the agricultural sector (i.e., increased productivity in the agricultural sector is not to be distributed in this sector, but rather it could be used to support the transferred labor). These assumptions will produce a net outflow from the agricultural sector if it would be possible to capture the agricultural surplus. Thus it has been remarked that "this crucial problem of collecting the food seems to be solved in Soviet Russia by the system of collective farms. The word 'collective' has here a double meaning. The collective farm is not only a form of collective organization; it is above all an instrument for collection" (*ibid.*, pp. 38-39). See also W. A. Lewis, "Economic Development with Unlimited Supplies of Labor," *The Manchester School of Economic and Social Studies*, May, 1954, and his "Unlimited Labor: Further Notes," *ibid.*, January, 1958; G. Ranis and J. C. H. Fei, "A Theory of Economic Development," *American Economic Review*, September, 1961.
43. B. F. Hoselitz, "The Use of Historical Comparisons in the Study of Economic Development," in R. Aron and B. F. Hoselitz (eds.), *Social Development* (Paris: Mouton, 1965).

44. S. Ishikawa, *Economic Development in Asian Perspective* (Tokyo: Kinokuniya, 1967), p. 319.
45. H. Wald, *Taxation of Agricultural Land in Underdeveloped Economies* (Cambridge: Harvard, 1959), p. 62.
46. *Kompas*, Indonesian daily newspaper. Interview with the Minister of Transmigration and Cooperative.
47. E. Kemenes, "Agriculture as a Possible Source of Accumulation in African Developing Countries," *Studies on Developing Countries*, no. 41, Budapest, 1970. See also M. P. Rudloff, "L'économie Villageoise et la Theorie du développement économique," *Cahiers de l'ISEA*, December, 1964; M. S. Marc, *Zone Franc et décolonisation* (Paris: SEDES, 1964); René Dumont, *L'Afrique Noire est Mal Partie* (Paris: Seuil, 1962).
48. See FAO, *Production Yearbook*, 1969.
49. Calculated from *Yearbook for International Trade Statistics*, 1970, United Nations publication.
50. *Review of International Trade and Development*, 1970, Table 24, p. 42.
51. N. Rath and V. S. Patvardhan, *Impact of Assistance under P.L. 480 on Indian Economy* (London: Asia Publishing House, 1967).
52. C. Beringer, *The Use of Agricultural Surplus Commodities for Economic Development in Pakistan* (Karachi: Institute of Development Economics, 1964).
53. E. S. Mason, *Economic Development in India and Pakistan* (Cambridge: Center for International Affairs, Harvard, 1966), p. 53.
54. A. Maddison, *Economic Progress and Policy in Developing Countries* (New York: Norton, 1970), p. 134.
55. See, for example, Ohkawa and Rosovsky, "The Role of Agriculture in Modern Japanese Economic Development," p. 61.
56. *Economic Development in Asian Perspective*, p. 77.
57. *Ibid.*, pp. 70, 77.
58. *Economic Bulletin for Asia and the Far East*, November, 1957. See also *World Economic Survey*, 1959.
59. Ohkawa and Rosovsky, "A Century of Japanese Economic Growth," p. 54.
60. K. Kiga, "Characteristics of Japan's Economic Growth," *Studies on Developing Countries*, no. 18, Budapest, 1968, p. 3.
61. S. Ishikawa, "Direction of Technological Change in Agricultural Production in the ECAFE Region during the 1970's," in *Development Prospects and Planning for the Coming Decade* (with

Special Report of the Fifth Interregional Seminar on Development Planning) (New York: United Nations, 1971), document ST/TAO/SER.C/133.

62. *Economic Development in Asian Perspective*, pp. 181-82.

63. See A. O. Hirschman, *Journeys Toward Progress* (New York: Twentieth Fund, 1963).

64. N. H. Jacoby, *U.S. Aid to Taiwan* (New York: Praeger, 1966), p. 199.

65. L. Solis, "Mexican Economic Policy in the Post-War Period: The Views of Mexican Economists," *American Economic Review*, June, 1971, Supplement, p. 13.

66. See K. N. Raj, "Some Questions Concerning Growth, Transformation and Planning in Agriculture in Developing Countries," *Journal of Development Planning*, No. 1 (United Nations publication, Sales No. E.69.II.B.24), pp. 21-25.

67. Permitting more intensive use of land through irrigation, supplies of power, road construction, mechanization, and better yields; throughout the postwar period, the growth rates of agricultural output per farm worker have been considerably higher than the developing countries' average. These two countries are also unlike other developing countries in terms of their growth in agricultural exports. Taiwan has a relatively easy access to Japan's market and could increase the exports of bananas, pineapples, mushrooms, and asparagus. Israel has expanded the exports of poultry, eggs, citrus, and oranges.

68. T. W. Schultz, *Transforming Traditional Agriculture* (New Haven: Yale, 1964).

69. Solis, *op. cit.*, pp. 11-13.

70. *Ibid.*, p. 13.

71. *Ibid.*, p. 13.

72. *Ibid.*, p. 14.

73. *Ibid.*, p. 13.

74. According to Raj, the seven states within the North and Pacific North regions, an area largely unaffected by the ceilings on the size of agricultural land holdings imposed by earlier land reforms, have accounted for 85 percent of the increase in the total value of the output of cotton and wheat in the two decades of 1939-59 (*op. cit.*, p. 19).

75. W. W. Hicks, *The Agricultural Development of Mexico, 1940-1960* (unpublished dissertation, Food Research Institute, Stanford University, October, 1965), quoted in Raj, *op. cit.*, p. 21.

76. Raj., *op. cit.*, p. 21.

CHAPTER IV

MEASURES OF THE LEVEL OF ECONOMIC DEVELOPMENT

The concept of development, and accordingly the level and the stage of development, has generally been considered as readily apparent although it is difficult to define. In fact it is an extremely complex question. Attempts, however, have been made to give its meaning a scientific content by resorting to devices involving the use of statistical indicators and criteria.

The most often quoted and the one considered to represent the single singificant index of the level of development is per capita income. According to the interpretation of the Committee for Development Planning, per capita gross domestic product is "a rough and ready indicator of the productive capacity of an economy and of its ability to provide needed services," although "it does not fully reflect such major condition of development as income redistribution or structural change."[1] The Economic Commission of Africa, on the other hand, has suggested the following reasoning: in an economy where "all resources were fully and efficiently used, productive capacity could be measured by gross domestic product"; although "no economy achieves full resource utilization and maximum efficiency," it can "be argued that gross domestic product is, in principle, an excellent *de facto* revelation of development levels."[2] The *"per capita* income statistic, for all its deficiencies, provides some measure of available productive capacity."[3] This point is important, it has been argued further, both because "there is a strong presumption that there will be some significant correlation between productive capacity and levels of development more widely construed, and because existing productive capacity is a powerful determinant of the options open to any given country at any point in time."[4] And "indeed, in a basic sense, the main problem of development is to increase this capacity."[5]

There are problems which arise from the use of per capita income as a measure of the level of development, for intercountry as well as for intertemporal comparisons within a country. First is definitional in nature, i.e., which concept of income to use. Secondly, it is statistical, due to differences in purchasing power, price structure, taste, and need.

Defects arising from these two problems are merely technical in nature and in principle they could be attenuated. Of more importance is the fact that the ability to measure does not necessarily correspond to the capability to grasp the significance of what is thus measured.

Per Capita Income: Some Notes on Its Economic Meaning

Production consists of the output of goods and services. The total output of goods and services within the confines of the geographical area of a country is defined as gross domestic product (GDP). GDP can be measured at factor cost or at market prices; the difference between the two concepts is the inclusion of indirect taxes net of subsidies in the latter. From a sample of selected developing countries, the ratios of GDP at factor cost to GDP at market prices range from 80 percent in Israel to 95 percent in Venezuela.[6]

It may be noted that in the developing countries, gross domestic product is usually produced through the help of foreign-owned capital and foreign manpower; both concepts of GDP do not take into account the compensation paid to these factors of production, nor adjustment made to compensation received from supplying factor services abroad. Gross national product (GNP), on the other hand, is the market value of the product attributable to the factors of production supplied by normal residents of the given country. Its difference with GDP at market prices is the net factor incomes received from abroad. In a sample of selected developing countries, GNP for 1967 is lower than GDP at market prices by between 1 percent in Ceylon to 28 percent in Liberia; exceptions are observed (whereby GNP is higher) in Jordan, Lebanon, Lesotho, Malawi, Republic of Korea, and Upper Volta.[7]

GNP, however, merely takes into account the net outflow of factor income whose magnitude may alter depending on the rule governing such outflow. Thus, for example, reinvested and undistributed profits by foreign-owned corporations as well as incomes of unincorporated foreign enterprises and resident expatriates may still be included in the concept. GNP, therefore, does not necessarily indicate the output attributable to the country's own citizens.

It has been observed that for the years 1960-63 foreign enterprise profits and settler or expatriate incomes exceeded one-third of domestic product in the following economies: Angola, Cameroon, Gabon, Libya, Mozambique, Guinea (Portuguese), Rhodesia, South Africa, South West Africa, Swaziland, and Zambia.[8] Algeria, Zaire, and Kenya were also in this group prior to independence.

An immediate problem which arises is whether undertaking an international income comparison is, in effect, comparing the comparables. Purchasing power, price structure, tastes, and needs differ between countries; the exchange rates utilized in converting values expressed in terms of national currencies into some common standard

unit merely reflect the relative purchasing powers for
internationally traded items and not of all goods and
services. Efforts have been made to achieve better international comparability by adjusting exchange rates for
differences in purchasing power as well as taking needs
into account.[9]

Needless to say, different methods of adjustment yield
different results; by way of illustration, it can be noted
that the ratio of per capita GDP in the United Kingdom
and Thailand has been reduced from 14:1 to 8:1 while
another estimate has reduced the ratio of their per capita
incomes from 14:1 to 2.5:1.[10]

If data were comparable, the results of comparisons
might depend on the period chosen. Developing countries
are often prone to balance of payments difficulties: the
results of comparison made at the time of devaluation
could significantly differ compared to the ones made prior
to the devaluation. While the use of the latest data has the
advantage of giving the most recent picture, it does not
necessarily assure the best comparability. Furthermore,
there is also a problem of whether the use of point
estimates is more appropriate than utilizing average of
estimates over a number of years.

If figures were comparable, and the time period chosen
does not significantly distort the results of international
income comparisons, a definitional problem which can be
considered is which concept of income to utilize. The
following table illustrates the effect of utilizing the
above-mentioned different concepts of income in the case
of two African countries, viz., Ghana and Liberia.

RATIO OF INCOME FIGURES: GHANA TO LIBERIA

Income *per capita*	1958	1963	1965	1966	1967	1968
GDP (factor cost)	104	87	98	106	83	75
GDP (market prices)	109	90	104	105	85	78
GNP	135	122	143	149	116	106

(in percent, Liberia = 100)

Source: Yearbook of National Accounts Statistics, 1969, Vols. I and II.

It can be seen from the above table that GNP in Ghana for all the years chosen is always higher than in Liberia; such an observation, however, cannot be made if instead, the gross domestic products were to be compared.

The difficulties arising from the statistical estimate could, in principle, be eased through methodological and data improvement while the appropriate concept to be utilized depends on the purpose of the comparison. More serious is the problem of interpretation, i.e., what economic content should be assigned to the statistical figures. If *per capita* GDP is to be interpreted as a measure of comparative levels of development as suggested above, then quantitatively, depending on the time period to be chosen, Ghana, as compared to Liberia, could fluctuate between higher and lower levels of development.

On the other hand, it has been observed qualitatively that "the Liberian economy is, except for its plantation and mining enclaves, relatively primitive, whereas that of Ghana is sufficiently developed for inter-industry analysis to be of some interest in planning."[11] In reference to Liberia furthermore, it has been noted that ". . . those changes in economic and social structure . . . are simply insufficient to transform the economy."[12] Although the country "has one of the highest rates of output growth on record because of heavy European and American investments in iron-ore, mining and rubber," it has been suggested that "Liberia must be placed among the least developed countries in Africa."[13] It is also interesting to note that in comparing two African countries with a large disparity in their per capita incomes, it has been observed that "Gabon with its $600 per capita GDP is not less but more underdeveloped than Rwanda with $70, in the sense that the structural characteristics of underdevelopment (dislocation and sectoral disparities in productivity) are more marked in Gabon."[14]

In this connection it may be further noted that roughly 22 developing countries have higher *per capita* GDP than Turkey, a developed economy in the United Nations classification of countries.[15] If *per capita* GDP were to be interpreted as an index of development level, by 1968, Libya, for example, is more developed than the United Kingdom since *per capita* GDP in Libya is greater by about 8 percent.[16] It appears, therefore, that the distinction between the developing and the developed countries which is solely based on *per capita* income contains a somewhat arbitrary element.

A factor which further complicates the interpretation of the meaning of *per capita* GDP is the pattern of ownership of the factors of production which directly affects factor earnings. *Per capita* GDP to be interpreted as reflecting an economy's ability to provide needed services begs the further question of "services for whom?" In Zaire, prior to independence (1958), the European population (which is less than 1 percent of the total) commanded 34 percent of the national income (exclusive of undistributed profits of European-owned companies).[17] In Kenya shortly after independence (1965), the average annual wage earnings of employees were markedly different for different ethnic groups.[18]

The effect of different patterns of ownership of the factors of production on the levels of *per capita* income can be most clearly seen from the East African data prior to independence. If *per capita* GDP were to be utilized as a measure, Kenya is the highest, Tanganyika the lowest, and Uganda in-between. On the other hand, if *per capita* African income were to be considered instead, the picture will change: Uganda is the highest, Kenya the lowest, and Tanganyika in-between.[19]

Thus, it appears that the use of *per capita* GDP as a measure of development level requires the acceptance of a postulate that all that matters is the level of GDP, and not how the process of production has occurred, nor does it matter who is in control of its production. In the developed countries, this kind of complexity might not arise since in most of these countries the factors of production are under the ownership and control of their own nationals.

Per Capita Income: Dramatization of an Illusion

Consider, for expository purposes, a tropical island economy, Fantasiana, whose main source of income is derived from fishing. Its per capita gross domestic product had been stagnant for decades, so that in the parlance of the previous discussions, its level of development has not increased. Although modern gadgets such as televisions and refrigerators had not been known to the populace (which, in other countries, had already been considered as basic necessities), wants and the means of their satisfaction were balancing each other. There had been an orderly social balance; within the given value system and according to their own understanding of happiness, people had on the whole been quite happy. In fact, there had been a spirit of mutual help and cooperation and no one felt alienated.

One day, a government sent a study mission to Fantasiana. The mission was shocked to find the miserably wretched living condition of the people in Fantasiana and it elaborated its assessment on this aspect in its report. Impressed by the efficiency of modern fishery abroad, it recommended that the only way to alleviate mass poverty rampant among the people of Fantasiana was through the inflow of foreign capital for developing its fishing industry. Given the abundance of fish within its territorial waters as well as the international waters surrounding the island, it was not difficult to attract foreign capital.

Fantasiana then negotiated foreign credit on its own behalf in order to build the lacking infrastructure (modern port facilities, road, electricity, etc.), constituting the basic prerequisites for attracting foreign investment. Foreign aid was easy in coming and after the completion of the infrastructure, foreign companies moved in with their huge trawlers and modern fishing equipment. Within one year, the amount of fish caught tripled although subsequently, with the larger base, its rates of growth were not as fast.

The foreign companies also found it profitable to invest in manufacturing plants of fish canning and fish by-products. From a negligible level, the share of manufacturing in gross domestic product subsequently reached 35 percent. Partly through foreign credits, Fantasiana was able to secure token ownership of the manufacturing industries though not the control of the decision making.

Within the decade, the rate of growth of gross domestic product was averaging at an annual rate of 22.5 percent, its per capita rate at 20 percent. Exports, which started from nothing, grew at an average annual rate of 39 percent. The speed of structural change and the rates of growth are impressive by any standard of intercountry and intertemporal comparisons.

A doctoral candidate was writing a dissertation on the economy. With mathematical precision he found the perfect fit for the time path of the growth profile of the manufacturing industries. He was able to trace the backward and forward linkages and offer a hypothesis regarding the leading sector. There was a highly significant correlation coefficient relating foreign capital inflow and the industrial development. He was able to complicate the Cobb-Douglas production function with statistically significant parameter estimates.

With gratifying exhilaration for his success in fitting facts to theoretical constructs, he wrote the dissertation, which also included projections of the economy based on past parametric estimates. Among the articulate jargons understandable only to people raised in the econometric artifact, he could not conceal his glee and admiration for the fantastic performance of the economy of Fantasiana and its bright future prospects, proceeding with policy prescriptions for other developing countries which are at a similar level to Fantasiana's earlier stage of development.

Behind the façade the hard-working fishermen who formerly had been the backbone of Fantasiana's economy were all driven out of competition and displaced. Small-scale ship-building was no longer needed and the workshops closed. Some were lucky enough to obtain jobs in the foreign companies which gave generous wages, salaries, and bonuses, in amounts considerably higher than they had ever dreamt; some became the servants of the foreigners and the emerging indigenous *nouveaux riches*; the majority, however, had to fall back on their families or became idly unemployed. The rise in per capita gross domestic product and the shift in the distribution of income also resulted in greater demand for imports partly substituting for domestic production since now it was a mark of inferiority to consume the products of domestic handicraft, creating more unemployment.

Fantasiana became acquainted with the sign of affluence together with the statistics of disguised and hard-core unemployment. It became the master in complicating the bureaucracy to secure payoffs so that money was the key word for services rendered, even to the poor. It also became intimately familiar with the emergence of crime and the dark sides of human nature. There was a growing tendency toward political and social stratification, where the consolidation of power was edging toward the elite, whose source of power was solely based on the economic advantage as the privileged beneficiary of the foreign enterprises.

There had been no alienation in misery; there was now political and social alienation in affluence. Naturally, the indigenous affluent looked with contempt on the apparently indolent poor. When the dissertation was criticized for ignoring the disruption in the social fabrics and the human values, the criticism was predictably dismissed as irredeemably irrelevant.

On one unfortunate day it became clear that the fishing resources were already depleted and it was no longer profitable for the foreign companies to continue their operation and so they pulled out of Fantasiana. No one had ever thought about this eventuality during the euphoric atmosphere of the high growth rates. Besides, cost-benefit analyses had persuaded the rich to invest in hotels, nightclubs, etc., none in manufacturing industries. The country was left with impressive modern offices and factories which became idle for lack of alternative uses; with a plethora of misfits who could not find their place in the changed society; and with the need to default on its past debt and interest payments while in the name of democracy, individual freedom, and liberty, the affluent managed to deposit their money in bank accounts abroad.

In this case, per capita gross domestic product and its growth as measures of development level and performance, are nothing but an illusion. The "miraculous" progress in economic performance was followed by moral, political, and social bankrupticies, and subsequently by economic bankruptcy as well.

The Level of Development: Extension of a Single Variable Concept

The use of per capita income as a measure of the level of development has an advantage of simplicity: since only one variable is involved, there is no statistical problem of weighting. Besides, its data are readily available and often have been scrutinized by international organizations. Notwithstanding the arguments in favor of its utilization, apparently it is not a sufficient index to represent the level of development. In practice, there is an air of arbitrariness in the distinction between developed and developing countries if solely based on this index: there are countries, which despite their high per capita income, are still considered and identified as developing.[20]

There has been a growing recognition that the use of per capita income is subject to justifiable criticisms and that the figure does not cover all the aspects of development. Accordingly there have been attempts to approach realism: the level of development is thus measured by per capita income and the addition of other relevant variables. Thus, for example, the United Nations Research Institute for Social Development has conducted an empirical study and has produced a "development index" from a combination of eighteen highly interrelated variables chosen from among seventy-three developmental and structural indicators covering social, demographic, and economic aspects.[21] The UNCTAD Secretariat has obtained the "level of development" indicator from six variables encompassing economic, social, and trade aspects.[22] The concept of the level of development, therefore, is defined as a composite index formed by a set of indicators.

The use of more than one variable to form a composite index involves the statistical problem of assigning the weight to each of the variables; factor analysis method, on the other hand, involves a process which yields an implicit weighting. Regardless of whether or not the statistical problem of weighting will arise, however, the conceptual problem has to be taken care of first: all the variables to be introduced should constitute elements of the concept of the level of development.

It may be noted that factor analysis, like any other statistical analysis, does not define a concept. At best the analysis provides the quantitative expression to the concept, but does not actually define it: the quantification is justifiable only if there is already a prior knowledge of what constitutes the level of development which is amenable to quantitative transformation, without which there will be a distinct possibility for specification error.[23] While it does not define a concept, the validity of the conceptual framework will determine whether its results will mislead or are useful. It serves a limited purpose only, i.e., classifying countries in accordance with their composite indices ranking.[24] It should be noted also that the enlargement of the number of variables will open the risk of greater observation error.[25] In short, it does not seem to be clear as yet whether its complexity, its level of sophistication, and the corresponding additional efforts needed are all commensurate with the results to be expected.

NOTES

1. See Official Records of the Economic and Social Council, Fifty-first Session, Supplement No. 7 (Document E/4990). Para. 58. The "Report of the ad hoc Group of Experts on special measures in favour of the least developed among the developing Countries" (UNCTAD document TD/B349) has noted that "it might prefer data concerning per capita GNP rather than GDP, to the extent available, because of the varying amounts that are transferred abroad as factor payments. It has also been noted that data concerning GNP originating in the monetized part of the economy might be considered as an indicator in the future" (p. 9).
2. See *A Survey of Economic Conditions in Africa*, 1969, Part II (United Nations publication, Sale No. E.71.II.K.6), p. 14.
3. *Loc. cit.*
4. *Ibid.*, p. 2.
5. *Loc. cit.* It has been suggested that "whether top priority is attached to Bible or beer, the Koran or the kitchen, leisure or lentils, rising average incomes are the means of attaining more of whatever the people in any society want." See Benjamin H. Higgins, *Economic Development* (London: 1968), p. 34.
6. See *World Economic Survey, 1969-1970* (United Nations publication, Sales No. E.71.II.C.1), table 3, p. 14.
7. *Loc. cit.*
8. R. H. Green and Ann Seidman, *Unity or Poverty?* (Baltimore: Penguin Books, 1968), p. 34.
9. See Colin Clark, *The Conditions of Economic Progress*, 3d ed. (London: Macmillan, 1957); M. Gilbert and M. Kravis, *An International Comparison of National Products and the Purchasing Power of Currencies* (Paris: OEEC, 1954); E. E. Hagen, "Some Facts about Income Levels and Economic Growth," *The Review of Economics and Statistics*, May, 1961; S. Kuznets, *Modern Economic Growth: Rate, Structure and Spread* (New Haven: Yale, 1966); W. Beckerman and R. Bacon, "International Comparisons of Income Levels," *Economic Journal*, December, 1966; V. Stoikov, "International Comparisons of Income Levels," *Economic Journal*, December, 1967. See also M. Gilbert et al., *Comparative National Products and Price Levels* (Paris: OEEC, 1958); Economic Commission for

Latin America, "The Measurement of Latin American Real Incomes in U.S. Dollars," *Economic Bulletin of Latin America*, October, 1967; S. N. Braithwaite, "Real Income Levels in Latin America, *Review of Income and Wealth*, June, 1968.

10. See A. Maddison, *Economic Progress and Policies in Developing Countries* (New York: W. W. Norton and Company, 1970), and D. Usher, "The Transport Bias in Comparisons of National Income," *Economics*, May, 1963.

11. P. Robson and D. A. Lury (eds.), *The Economies of Africa* (London: George Allen and Unwin, 1969), pp. 23-24.

12. G. Dalton, "History, Politics and Economic Development in Liberia," *Journal of Economic History*, December, 1965, pp. 581-82. See also R. Clower et al., *Growth without Development: An Economic Survey of Liberia* (Evanston: Northwestern University Press, 1966).

13. G. Dalton and A. A. Walters, "The Economies of Liberia," in Robson and Lury, *The Economies of Africa*, pp. 287 and 314.

14. S. Amin, "Development and Structural Change: The African Experience, 1950-1970," *Journal of International Affairs*, vol. XXIV, no. 2, 1970, p. 217. It can be noted that the United Nations estimates for *per capita* GDP (at current market prices) in Gabon and Rwanda for the year 1967 were, respectively, $504 and $46 *(World Economic Survey, 1969-1970*, pp. 177-78).

15. Cf. *Handbook of International Trade and Development Statistics*, supplement 1970 (United Nations publication, Sales No. E/F.70.II.D.12), table 6.11.

16. Calculated from the *Yearbook of National Accounts Statistics*, 1969, vol. II (United Nations publication, Sales No. E.71.XVII.3), table 1B.

17. See F. Bezy, "Problems of Economic Development of the Congo," in E. A. G. Robinson (ed.), *Economic Development for Africa South of the Sahara* (New York: St Martin's Press, 1964), table 11, p. 84.

18. In all sectors, the ratios of Asian and European to African earnings for the year 1965 are 5:1 and 13:1, respectively. In the agriculture and forestry sector only, the ratios are, respectively, 14:1 and 31:1; African average annual wage earnings in this sector are less than half of that for all sectors. Prior to independence (1959), the ratios of Asian and European to African earnings were 8:1 and 19:1, respectively. The figures are

calculated from J. B. K. Hunter, "The Development of the
Labor Market in Kenya," in I. G. Stewart, *Economic Develop-
ment and Structural Change* (Edinburgh: Edinburgh University
Press, 1969), table 2, p. 119, and D. Walker, "Problems of
Economic Development of East Africa," Statistical Appendix in
Robinson.

19. See B. Van Arkadie and D. Ghai, "The East African Econo-
    mies," table 3, p. 324, in Robson and Lury (eds.), *The
    Economies of Africa.*

20. See Gunnar Myrdal, *Asian Drama*, 3 vols. (New York: The
    Twentieth Century Fund, 1968), vol. I, pp. 474-84. Thirty-eight
    of these indicators are social and demographic, the rest are
    economic in nature. See United Nations Research Institute for
    Social Development, *Contents and Measurement of Socio-
    Economic Development: An Empirical Enquiry* (Geneva, 1970)
    (report no. 70.10).

21. Three of these variables refer to economic, two to social, and
    one to trade, aspects. See "Identification of the Least De-
    veloped among the Developing Countries," Report by the
    UNCTAD Secretariat, July 11, 1969 (Document TD/B/269),
    p. 13.

22. Cf. *ibid.*, para. 15, p. 4. See also Irma Adelman and Cynthia T.
    Morris, *Society, Politics and Economic Development—A Quan-
    titative Approach* (Baltimore: The Johns Hopkins Press, 1967),
    and J. Eckstein, *Quantitative Measure of Development Perfor-
    mance*, University of Michigan, Center for Research and
    Economic Development, Discussion Paper No. 7.

23. It is quite possible, for example, to obtain a composite index
    from the number of nightclubs, traffic accidents, suicide rate,
    coronary disease, and ulcer per adult population, content of
    carbon monoxide in the atmosphere, etc. (all probably corre-
    lated to economic development), but whether the results would
    be useful is not clear. Thus, resorting to factor analysis still
    opens the question regarding the particular variables to be
    presumed as external manifestation of a common underlying
    factor considered to represent the level of development.
    Furthermore, the concept of the level of development may
    contain some qualitative elements which defy quantification
    and accordingly do not enter into the analysis regardless of their
    importance.

24. It does not, however, specify the probability of misclassifica-

tion, and neither does it assist in deciding on the proper demarcation lines for country groupings. In a dynamic sense, it presupposes that a country can raise its level of development only if it improves its position relative to others within the sample; in other words, if there exists at least one country which does not perform as well. For, if in each and every country all the variables entering into the model grow in such a way as to maintain their respective ranking, the level of development of a particular country so defined does not change regardless of its observed growth.

25. It may be noted that covering the maximum number of statistical indicators for intercountry comparisons could seriously curtail the sample size for lack of data availability and comparability. It would also involve considerable additional work in analyzing the quality of the individual series as well as in making adjustments for their comparability.

CHAPTER V

ECONOMIC THEORY
AND DEVELOPMENT
Problems and Application

The Relative Meaning of Development

It appears from the previous discussions that regardless of whichever criteria one would prefer to utilize in identifying a developing country, he is bound to face the relative nature of the concept. If this proposition is accepted, it would be meaningless to seek an exhaustive and unambiguous definition of the level of development. All that could be expected is that when the need arises, there are some operationally useful criteria for its identification.

In some cases per capita income would suffice while in other cases it might need to be supplemented by other variables. In all cases, however, it does not seem likely that the application of the criteria would yield results which are devoid of arbitrariness and which are unambiguous. This seems to be inevitable as long as the developing countries as they are known now are characterized more by their diversity than by their homogeneity.

Notwithstanding the euphemistic terms which have been invented in order to avoid the unfavorable connotations engendered by the term, developing countries are those which are at the stage of underdevelopment, i.e., those which are not yet developed. Comparison and contrast to the developed economies, therefore, are the essence of the concept. It is essentially a negative concept: it characterizes that which they are not but does not positively specify what in fact they are.

It may be said that the developed economies possess a number of common characteristics by which they can be identified. To mention a few: relatively high per capita income; modern and industrialized production systems, where there exist numerous and significant intersectoral relationships; the economies are nationally integrated, flexible, and capable of self-generated and self-sustained growth; international trade may be important but not crucial; foreign ownership and control of the factors of production may exist, but may not be pervasive, so they have the relative strength and ability to determine the course of domestic economic events on their own terms and on the bases of their own national interest.

By contrast, none of the foregoing characteristics is fully and directly applicable to the developing countries; in fact, probably the precise opposites apply to the majority of these countries.[1] The degree and extent of the opposite characteristics to be found among the developing countries, however, are far from homogeneous as to warrant the specification of an exhaustive common denominator.

A state of underdevelopment may be regarded as a state of deficiencies: relatively low per capita income; lack of diversification in the economic activities; predominance of agriculture and the absence or insufficiency of industrial activities; relatively low labor productivity even in the agricultural sector; lack of technological, administrative, managerial, and organizational know-how to ensure a certain kind and level of economic performance and social well-being; vulnerability to the vagaries of international market conditions; small size of the monetized sector, a greater part of which may be owned and/or controlled by foreigners. Not the least important is the fact that the relative structural weaknesses may lead to the state of relative dependence on outside powers even in the determination of the course of national economic events.

Again it must be emphasized that these deficiencies do not define underdevelopment; they are merely an enumeration of a deficient state of affairs. For each and every one of the deficiencies which can be transformed into quantitative variables, its state of underdevelopment can be measured by the distance to the developed state. However, the linear combination of the scalers can be regarded as an index of the general state of underdevelopment if and only if all the scalers represent the state of underdevelopment and are not merely correlated with it.

Development, on the other hand, may be viewed as a process in attenuating the state of deficiencies. It is a process for the betterment. Although not each and every one of the deficiencies is quantifiable, among those which are, the process can be represented by their rates of growth. Theoretically, if the index of the general state of underdevelopment can be satisfactorily constructed, the whole process of development can be inferred from the comparison of the two indices at two different points of time.

This assumes, however, that the process of development is a simple technical problem which can be dealt with by the usual problem-solving technique.[2] In fact, the problem may involve normative questions as well regarding what constitutes an element of betterment.[3] For example, to take only two variables, viz., per capita income and the state of economic dependence.

Within a given period of time, a greater per capita income might be compatible with an increase in the degree of economic dependence while a greater degree of economic independence might be incompatible with an increase in per capita income. The state of compatibility might yield a better index than the state of incompatibility: however, only in the absence of a normative judgment could it be said that the former is better.

Thus, the measurement of a development process is hazardous for the following reasons. First, the conceptual difficulties attending the measurement of the state of underdevelopment. Second, even if the conceptual difficulties could be overcome, there are normative elements entering into the picture (in principle, these elements could be incorporated by assigning different weights; these weights, however, are a matter of opinion, mitigating the scientific content of the measurement). Third, the state of underdevelopment is multifarious; the effects of attempts at attenuating the deficiencies might be observed differently according to the choice of the period of observation.

The meaning of development performance is, therefore, dependent on the concept of underdevelopment; it is affected by the opinion regarding the normative questions; and it is a function of the period of observation. In this sense, development performance is a relative achievement.

It is probably due to these difficulties that the rate of growth of per capita income has been used as a measure of development performance. However, as has been pointed out earlier, the interpretation of the meaning of per capita income figures in the developed countries cannot be considered in the same vein as in the developing countries. Accordingly, the use of its rate of growth as a measure of development performance by no means assumes an unambiguous meaning.

Application of Economic Theory in Economic Development

Although there is a substantial economic content in the notion of economic development, the addition of the qualifying adjective does not make the concept any more succinct. For, whether one or more variables are to be used as a measure, the problems referred to above will also be encountered. If the concept of economic development itself is not unambiguous, what will then be the contribution of economic theory in diagnosing and solving the problems related to economic development?[4]

It may be recalled that economics has been defined as

"the study of human behavior as a relationship between a multiplicity of ends and scarce means that have alternative uses."[5] The relationship between the multiplicity of ends and the limited means has yielded the efficiency postulate in economic theory: achieving a given end with the least use of means or, alternatively, obtaining a maximum end through the given use of means. In aggregate terms, the end is referred to as aggregate production, and the means as available resources or factors of production which facilitate the production to take place. Through the behavioral assumptions and the interaction of the individual preferences of producers, consumers, and owners of the factors of production, and given the existing distribution of wealth, perfect competition in all markets would lead to an optimal allocation of resources and maximum social welfare.[6]

In essence economic theory deals with problems of optimal allocation of resources to obtain the level of aggregate output which maximizes social welfare. The problem of increasing production as it involves the allocation of resources is dealt with by economic development theory for the developing countries, by economic growth theory for the developed economies.

Keynes has noted that the theory of economics does not furnish a body of settled conclusions immediately applicable to policy. It is a method rather than a doctrine, an apparatus of the mind, a technique of thinking, which helps its possessor to draw correct conclusions. Does the method really help to draw the correct conclusions as it is related to practical problems? Is the apparatus really conducive in framing the correct way of thinking, at least in directing the mind to ask the right questions, particularly with regard to the practical problems of the developing countries?

The danger of a technique, especially if it has a scientific pretense, is if it leads one to get bogged down to it; not only in drawing the logical deductions, but also in framing the questions to be asked. Instead of being its master one could become its slave. Rather than utilizing it to obtain better understanding of the complex reality, the latter is forced to conform to its requirements. On the other hand, the art of theorizing is to be able to reduce complex problems into a comprehensible and manageable system; occasionally, however, as a mark of sophistication, one is tempted to complicate an otherwise simple problem.

Recently, a concern was expressed in a Presidential Address to the Royal Economic Society regarding "the smallness of the contribution that the most conspicuous developments of economics in the last quarter of a century have made to the solution of the most pressing problems of the times."[7] Thus, "it is because I find this divergence between economics and practical problems increasingly a cause of disappointment and disquiet not only to those who have to tackle those problems, but also to those concerned with the advancement of economics as a science, that I have been moved to put the issue before the members of the Royal Economic Society."[8] It has been observed also that "it may even be that training in advanced economics is actively unhelpful. I find it is a common experience that when graduates in economics first assume practical responsibilities they have something to unlearn."[9]

If such a concern has arisen in the developed country, the problem deserves even more serious consideration for the developing economies. For, as has been noted above, the concept of developing countries essentially gives rise to the comparison and contrast to the developed ones, where most likely the structural characteristics to be found in the two groupings would be the precise opposites. Although it must be admitted that the treatment here is far from giving sufficient justice to the complexity of the problem, a few observations may be noted.

By nature of its discipline and its concern with efficiency, the determination of an optimal allocation of resources, whether in a *laissez-faire* or a centrally planned economy, is inevitably cast in terms of cost of input and value of output relationship; in other words, it relies on the price system. On the other hand, in the developing countries, markets are localized and regionalized, a substantial part of domestic product is from a subsistence or nonmonetized sector, and there are limits to factors mobility and substitutability, so that the price system cannot be completely relied upon. Besides, through government policy or otherwise, the existing price system may be distorted, for example, wage, interest, and foreign exchange rates may not actually reflect their true opportunity costs resulting in a situation whereby relative availability of factors of production and the factors proportions actually utilized in production are not necessarily in line.

It may be noted that the market-determined price system is partly formed by demand as expressed in the market place, reflecting individual "revealed preferences" under the given income and wealth distribution. Revealed preferences, however, do not ensure the availability of resources favorable for the increase in production, nor do they ensure that if the increase in production does in fact take place, it will be in the form which attenuates the structural deficiencies. With the growing importance of the government sector in the developing countries, revealed preferences assume a political dimension as well; the growing concern with the distribution of income (which economic analysis alone cannot cope with), on the other hand, results in the need to consider not only the political, but also the historical, sociological, and philosophical questions. It is not clear, therefore, whether economic analysis of economic development can afford to ignore noneconomic considerations.

Even in the best of circumstances of perfect competitive market conditions (which do not obtain in reality), the price system can lead to a perpetual or deteriorating state of structural deficiencies. For example, the price system can be used as a weapon to crush the ambition of a developing country to industrialize because a mass of data can be accumulated pointing to the folly of such enterprise on the ground of inefficiency, and the wisdom of maintaining the existing structure. In addition, the logic of resource allocation calls upon marginal analyses, a condition which is far apart from the context in which actual decisions must take place, most often discontinuous in nature, and where the smooth adjustments and the substitutability of the factors of production simply do not exist.

In a theoretical formulation, all the assumptions must be granted first before the argument begins.[10] An economist usually does not analyze without a theoretical model in mind; the model consists, among others, of specifications regarding economic behavior, institutional rules, and technological laws of transformation.[11] Since "knowledge is useful if it helps to make the best decisions,"[12] an economic model is useful to the developing countries if it does assist in formulating the best policies for attenuating their structural deficiencies.

Regarding the policy prescriptions so derived, it is quite possible that the prescriptions are right for the wrong reason, i.e., they work precisely because the assumptions underlying the model are not valid. In a theoretical discussion this possibility can be ruled out because bad theorizing will not gain currency. In practice, however, powerful economic doctrine may apply regardless of the relevance of the assumptions underlying the model from which the doctrine is drawn. This is particularly the case in international relations: "in each era the rules for international economic relations are molded to suit the views of the country that is then the most powerful."[13] Thus it has been argued that "the economist's case for free trade is deployed by means of a model from which all relevant considerations are eliminated by the assumptions. . . . Yet prescriptions for policy were drawn from it, with great confidence, to apply to a world which by no means conformed to the assumptions."[14] And "in practice the policy seemed to work, in the era that ended in 1914, just because the assumptions of the model were not fulfilled."[15] But "we ought not to be surprised that what now seems such a flimsy construction as the economists' model should have appeared to hold so much weight and authority, for it did not really have to stand on its own logical base. It was the facade of a dogma with solid interests behind it."[16]

Thus it has been observed that economists in the developed countries "have viewed matters too exclusively from the point of view of their own nations' circumstances and interests, which are not always those of the peoples in the underdeveloped countries."[17] And "it should not surprise us that, on the whole, the literature is curiously devoid of attempts to relate the facts of international inequalities and the problems of underdevelopment and development to the theory of international trade."[18] On the other hand, in an attempt to defend the classical and neoclassical position that international trade is not merely a device for achieving productive efficiency but constitutes an "engine of growth"[19] as well, it has been found necessary to suggest the following arguments.

The merging of the gains from trade with the gains from growth rests ultimately, therefore, on the efficacy of domestic policy measures in producing sufficient social and political change, as well as economic change, to make the economy more responsive to the stimulus from trade. If this is accomplished, the benefits of international specialization may then be secured not only for economic efficiency, but also for the urgent challenge of accelerating development.[20]

These arguments purport to show that the model will work if only the developing countries conform to the assumptions as applied in the developed economies. But developing countries are those which are not developed; the assumptions, therefore, need to be analyzed on their own terms and be the object of the analysis rather than its starting point of departure.

The view that international trade could propel development has been vindicated in many countries that are now among the developed: Denmark, Norway, Sweden, Switzerland, and the United Kingdom in Europe; Canada and the United States in North America; Japan[21] in Asia; and Australia. The historical context of the nineteenth-century world order, however, is not similar to the contemporary era. When growth took place, these countries were not under colonial domination such that in some instances the governments could pursue energetic policies for home market expansion and protect domestic industries, not in conformity with the free trade doctrine.

For their immediate usefulness to a particular developing country, models of economic growth are probably too abstract and general. They are mainly concerned with the intertemporal pattern of behavior of given economic relationships, assuming homogeneity of economies, where the economic variables are subject to laws of transformation which are universally applicable. The specifications of the economic relationships have originated from certain systems (based on the economic structure of the industrialized economies) whereby institutions, motivations, availability and mobility of resources as well as their substitutability are taken as given and conform to the situation to be found in the developed economies.

The models usually disregard the historical context and the level of development of any particular country, do not specify the initial conditions[22] encompassing complex political, social, and cultural problems in addition to those which are strictly economic. They assume away the dynamics of political and social changes and their interrealtionships with economic development. Specifications made purely in economic terms often make it appear that the noneconomic variables are somehow a nuisance, a recalcitrant deadweight, which impede an otherwise smooth efficient growth path which could easily be attained if only those factors behave as assumed. In short, the models presuppose underlying assumptions and restrictions which need to be analyzed on their own terms rather than being taken for granted and simply assumed. The usefulness of an economic model to a developing country is probably determined by the following factors: whether its explicit choice of problem is of particular importance; whether its underlying assumptions and specifications of relationships are relevant; and whether the policy prescriptions drawn from it serve the national interest of the country in question. If a model is too advanced, in the sense that its underlying assumptions and logical constructs presuppose conditions which are applicable .only to a developed country, then the hasty acceptance of its conclusion might lead to irrelevant or misleading policy formulation and could even be erroneous.

The blind acceptance of the "free-trade" and "trade as an engine of growth" doctrines, for example, might lead to a state of perpetual structural deficiencies. The problem of increasing per capita income might be important (and even crucial), but not in all circumstances will it serve the national interest. For the latter also requires a clear knowledge of who is in control of the process of production and its consequent distribution of income; of how production has been generated; and whether the increase in income is compatible with the attenuation of structural weaknesses. The reliance of economic theory on the price system has to be put in juxtaposition with the fact that in many developing countries markets are localized and not nationally integrated; that a substantial portion of domestic product originates from the subsistence or nonmonetized sector; that there are infant industries whose very existence requires the interference with the price mechanism; that there are limitations to factor availability, mobility, and substitutability.

The introduction of national interest in an economic model might rob it of its scientific and objective content. But it seems doubtful that if one is truly trying to attack the problem of underdevelopment, one could really retain a scientific and objective attitude since, as has been noted earlier, the development process involves normative judgment.

The president of the Royal Economic Society has suggested that the economist's studies should be "field-determined, not discipline-determined."[23] He has endorsed the view that "if there ever is another great synthetic statement to cover economics and its current problems of growth, then that new statement or theory will not be a general theory of economics alone, it will instead be a general theory of social affairs."[24]

A theory of economic development should probably not be dictated by the academic tradition of distinguishing economic and other factors, but by the need for alleviating the basic trauma of underdevelopment as it is related to a particular developing country. This is not too promising an area for producing a general theory, but given the fact that developing countries are by no means homogeneous, it can be questioned whether there exists a relevant and useful generalized theory of economic development.

It seems, however, that one thing could probably be broadly generalized: the politically independent developing countries are often characterized by a state of economic dependence, where effective economic decision and planning have to depend to various degrees, directly or indirectly, on the decisions of foreign governments, foreign-market conditions, and foreign-controlled or foreign-owned giant corporations whose resources sometimes considerably exceed those of the national governments they are dealing with. Economic dependence is the manifestation of the state of deficiencies: low income and lack of domestic resources (and the low capacity for their mobilization as well) necessitate the reliance of national development plans to some extent on foreign aid and foreign capital inflow; lack of diversification in economic activities results in the vulnerability to export proceeds; lack of nationally integrated industries results in foreign-market orientation in selling primary output and in buying input (capital goods, raw materials, spare parts), weakening the backward and forward linkages of industrialization process; lack of industrialization makes a country dependent on imports and foreign credits for controlling domestic inflationary pressures; the widening gap between foreign exchange receipts from exports and the requirements for imports produces an increasing need for foreign capital inflow; dependence on foreign financing may result in the adoption of capital-intensive technique in the face of growing unemployment; etc. Even in the field of agricultural products, some countries are dependent on foreign aid and assistance. Regardless of whether the foreign components produce good or bad effects on the national economy, a normative element could probably be suggested: the state of economic dependence is undesirable.

Richard M. Nixon, the President of the United States, in an address to the joint session of Canada's Parliament, recalled that the United States was dependent on European capital for its development prior to World War I, but was eager to terminate this dependence. And the American leader emphasized: "No self-respecting nation could or should accept the proposition that it should always be economically dependent upon another nation."

The central problem of any developing country is probably that of reducing the state of economic dependence. Given the complex constellation of factors in the developing countries, the long-term strategy of economic independence may necessitate the short-term tactics of economic dependence. It does not seem, however, that there exists an economic model which takes the reduction of the state of economic dependence as the central question of its inquiry; it is, of course, a much more complex problem than, say, the question of increasing per capita income.

NOTES

1. For a parallel discussion, see Reginald H. Green, *Stages in Economic Development: Changes in the Structure of Production, Demand and International Trade*, Yale University Economic Growth Center, Center Paper No. 125, 1969.

2. Note, for example, the following observation: "the Economics of development is not very complicated; the secret of successful planning lies more in sensible politics and good public administration." See W. Arthur Lewis, *Development Planning* (New York: Harper and Row, 1966), preface.

3. In strictly economic terms, an efficient solution is better than a less efficient one. Accordingly, with given equivalent efforts, one who earns more is better than one who earns less. Within a specified period of time, it is conceivable that a prostitute and a pantomime may have an equivalent man-hours work as commonly defined in economics, where the former earns considerably more even after discounting the costs of professional hazards. Regardless of the economic system being adopted, one would not probably hesitate to add normative values before deciding which of the two is better, arising from the fact that the distinguishing characteristic of human nature is its concern with human dignity. It may be argued, for example, that the postwar reversion of political independence to colonialization may in the short run increase per capita gross domestic product; however, it can be predicted confidently that no country which still respects the value of human dignity would opt for such a choice. There is then a question whether an increase in any development indicator should or should not be examined in the light of what it does to human dignity before deciding on whether or not there has been development.

4. It has been argued that during the last ten years there was no significant progress in theory. See Egbert DeVries, "A Review of Literature on Development Theory," in *International Development Review*, March, 1968.

5. Lionel Robbins, *An Essay on the Nature and Significance of Economic Science* (London: Macmillan, 1940), p. 16.

6. See Francis M. Bator, "The Simple Analytics of Welfare Maximization," *American Economic Review*, March, 1957, and his "The Anatomy of Market Failure," *Quarterly Journal of*

Economics, 1958. See, however, R. G. Lipsey and R. K. Lancaster, "The General Theory of Second Best," *Review of Economic Studies,* December, 1956.

7. E. H. Phelps Brown, "The Underdevelopment of Economics," *Economic Journal,* March, 1972, p. 1. The most conspicuous developments have been taken to be: the refinement of the logic of resource allocation and decision-taking; the building of growth models; and econometric analyses of systems of economic forces. On the other hand, the most pressing problems have been considered to be: fostering growth in poor countries, and improving the performance of the industrialized economies; adjusting the balance of payments; checking out inflation while maintaining full employment; deciding the scope of the free market and government intervention; checking the adverse effects on the environment and the quality of life of industrialism, population growth, and urbanism.

8. *Ibid.,* p. 2.

9. *Loc. cit.*

10. It is not necessary that the assumptions have to be verified first. For one can experiment by drawing out their implications, and then test whether the resulting formulation fits the observed facts. It has been suggested, however, that the usefulness of theory is not equal to its distinction for it is impaired by being built upon assumptions that are plucked from the air: "what does impair it, scientifically and practically, is that the human propensities and reactions it purports to abstract are not in fact abstracted, that is to say drawn out from observations, but are simply assumed" (*ibid.,* p. 3).

11. Econometric methodology has been crystallized so that specifications of functional relationships, expressed in terms of quantifiable variables, can be tested empirically either through cross-section or time-series analyses. Note, however, that "where, as so often, the fluctuations of different series respond in common to the pulse of the economy, it is fatally easy to get a good fit, and get it for quite a number of different equations. . . . Basically, we cannot get more knowledge of causality out of a statistical fit than we put into the behavioral equations that are fitted; these imply a certain flow of forces, and the outcome of identification procedures depends on what this flow has been assumed to be *a priori*" (*ibid.,* p. 6). As has been suggested by Marschak in one single sentence: "Thus,

practice requires theory." See Jacob Marschak, "Economic Measurements for Policy and Prediction," in W. C. Hood and Tjalling C. Koopmans (eds.), *Studies in Econometric Method* (New York: John Wiley, 1953), p. 26. See also Tjalling C. Koopmans, "Identification Problems in Economic Model Construction," in *ibid.*

12. *Ibid.*, p. 1.

13. Joan Robinson, *The New Mercantilism, An Inaugural Lecture* (Cambridge: Cambridge University Press, 1966), p. 25.

14. *Ibid.*, pp. 1-2.

15. *Ibid.*, p. 2.

16. *Ibid.*, p. 6.

17. Gunnar Myrdal, *An International Economy* (New York: Harper and Bros., 1956), p. 222.

18. Gunnar Myrdal, *Rich Lands and Poor* (New York: Harper and Bros., 1957), p. 154.

19. D. H. Robertson, "The Future of International Trade," reprinted in American Economic Association, *Readings in the Theory of International Trade* (Philadelphia: Blakiston, 1949), p. 501.

20. Gerald M. Meier, *International Trade and Development* (New York: Harper and Row, 1963), p. 191. The view is based on the theory of comparative advantage, a function of factor proportions (see also the Hecksher-Ohlin relative factor supply thesis in E. Hecksher, "The Effect of Trade on the Distribution of Income," in *Readings in the Theory of International Trade*, and B. Ohlin, *Interregional and International Trade* (Cambridge: Harvard University Press, 1933). On the other hand, it has been suggested that comparative advantage in manufactures is related to the level of development rather than to factor proportions [see S. Burenstam Linder, *An Essay on Trade and Transformation* (New York: John Wiley, 1961)].

21. That Japan can be considered a case is "nothing but a literary invention." See W. W. Lockwood, *The Economic Development of Japan: Growth and Structural Change, 1868-1938* (Princeton: Princeton University Press, 1954).

22. For elaboration of differences in initial conditions of presently developed countries as compared to those of the developing countries, see, for example, Simon Kuznets, "Present Underdeveloped Countries and Past Growth Patterns," Eastin Nelson (ed.), *Economic Growth* (Austin: University of Texas Press,

1960). For the Asian context, see S. Ishikawa, *Economic Development in Asian Perspective.*

23. "The Underdevelopment of Economics," p. 7.
24. M. J. Fores, "No More General Theories?," *Economic Journal,* March, 1969, p. 19.

CHAPTER VI

MAN AND ECONOMIC
DEVELOPMENT

Many of the developing countries were under colonial tutelage for a long period of time. To a large measure the pattern of growth in these countries reflects the past role of colonial policy in promoting trade and certain kinds of international specialization. Previously these colonies were in certain types of primitive stationary states where wants and means of gratification were in balance according to their subsistent needs.[1]

Subsequently there was an impetus which brought these colonies into the exchange economies, and was further enhanced after the consolidation of colonial control was able to secure law and order, provision of transportation networks, and utilization of uniform currencies. Thus, two distinct sectors were created: on the one hand was the subsistence or traditional while on the other was the modern, exchange, or monetary sector.[2]

Needless to say, the two sectoral distinctions are not very precise, but rather serve as a mere approximation; in fact, the dichotomy has been criticized as offering no operational guide for comprehensive development policy.[3] However, the dichotomy can be regarded as extremes in a continuum spectrum. Thus, for example, the spectrum might be composed of purely subsistent production with a small production for the market; mostly for the market with some production for direct consumption; and specialized production for the market or completely monetized sector.[4]

Further refinements could be made by introducing the concept of ownership. The various forms of differentiation might be further collapsed into a three-sectoral model, thereby introducing a concept of a plural economy consisting of subsistence, indigenous money economy, and foreign-enclave sectors. The essence of the various forms of distinction is that unlike the developed, the developing countries through historical heritage have weak intersectoral relations in their domestic economy.

In some colonies the original impetus of the monetized sector originated from mineral discoveries, while in others it came from the introduction of crops for exports. While the former was exclusively owned by a nonindigenous population during the colonial period, there were two patterns which emerged from the latter, viz., one where the cash crops were mainly, though not necessarily exclusively, produced by the indigenous population, and another where the crops came from nonindigenously owned and managed plantations and large farms.

From the production side, the growth in the monetary sector has the effect of changing the economic structure, followed by fossilization in the new pattern resulting in a sort of international specialization based on comparative advantage of mineral resources, local unskilled labor, and tropical climate, where the transformation into exportable raw materials was performed through nonindigenous capital and management. From the demand side, it created new tastes and new patterns of demand. On the supply and demand sides, the orientation was toward foreign markets, creating a situation of economic dependence.

It may be noted that in the presently developed economies, the initial impetus originated from agriculture, mining, or the production of raw materials for exports. The main catalyst of industrialization in the United States during the period 1820-40, for example, was cotton exports.[5] There is, however, one fundamental difference: whereas the growth in money income from exports generated expansion in the secondary and the tertiary sectors of the presently developed economies, in the colonies the new tastes and demand were largely met through imports and the colonial commercial policy allowed hardly any scope for developing domestic industry.

In contrast to the United States, for example, which had relied on tariff protection for the development of the domestic industries, the textile industry in India was able to withstand competition from Manchester only in the crudest products such as cotton yarn. The subsequent growth of exports and imports in the colonies led to the development of a new class: the middlemen who acted as the go-between for the large European trading corporation and the indigenous population, frequently performing the functions of money-lenders as well, and who were very often nonindigenous.

Activities related to trade, industry, finance, transport, distribution of imports as well as processing of exports were largely under the control of the nonindigenous population. In East Africa prior to independence, for example, non-Africans owned and controlled almost all the wholesale trade and a good deal of the retail trade, industrial as well as financial services, and filled most of the technical positions and senior administrative posts in the public services. The range of opportunities within the reach of the indigenous population was largely limited to traditional farming and menial work in mining, plantations, and service sectors, junior clerks and administrative officials, and low-grade teachers; the development of a stable and skilled labor force was thwarted and very little diffusion of skills was taking place.[6] Where domestic entrepreneurship appeared, it could be discouraged; where it had existed, it might be curtailed or eliminated.[7]

Thus, while export growth in the presently developed

economies had produced nationally integrated economies capable of self-generating and self-sustained growth, the previously colonized and recently independent countries have instead inherited foreign enclaves and an indigenous monetary sector with generally weak linkage effects to the domestic economy, in addition to the probably stationary subsistent sector. Two extremes in the spectrum of economic structures of recently independent countries might, therefore, be suggested, between which their position might be placed.

On the one hand, there is an economy where the nonindigenous involvement in the economic activities is not very significant and production activities are predominantly left to the subsistence sector. Perhaps this is because the country is not particularly rich in natural resources, the location is too remote or isolated to permit the establishment of flourishing commercial and trading centers, or the climate is too harsh. On the other hand, there is an economy where various factors are conducive to intensive nonindigenous economic activities which lead to significant penetration in various sectors as well as a substantial degree of monetization of the economy. In the former, the forces of growth which could have been taken for granted elsewhere have probably not been institutionalized and in some cases would have to be introduced from scratch. In the latter, even if these forces are present, they may not be under the full control of the indigenous population and possibly little has been gained by the indigenous in mastering and assimilating modern technology, management, and organizational skills.

It should be emphasized, however, that the presence of colonial domination did not merely take the form of the grafting upon the colonies of European and nonindigenous enterprises while maintaining the basic characteristics of the society intact, as the proceeding discussions might appear to suggest. In Indonesia, and specifically in Java, it has been suggested that the impact of Dutch rule substantially altered the basic structure of Javanese social organization and to an appreciable extent also the political and economic attitudes.[8]

The peasantry which on the whole had possessed substantial economic strength before, became economically as well as politically weak. The Dutch utilized a system of indirect rule to secure the political control for attaining its economic objectives by using the Javanese aristocratic elite as its agent; the *quid pro quo* for its serving as an instrument was not only political (the readiness of the Dutch to use its military force to back the elite against the populace) but also economic, whereby it was given a free hand in squeezing out the villages.

Prior to the arrival of the Dutch, Chinese merchants had already been active on the north coast of Java; their activities, however, had been confined to being intermediaries, largely on a wholesale basis. With the arrival of the Dutch, they changed into becoming intermediaries between the Dutch and the population of Java. At first it was largely confined to the retailing of imports, but subsequently they were also engaged in the gathering of the native produce for export; since the political constellation assured the repayment from local villages, they also practiced usury, imposing onerous conditions.

The introduction of various taxes payable in money forced the peasantry to obtain cash; invariably the peasants had to borrow from the local money-lenders, who in most cases were their only source of credit and were usually Chinese. Often because of his inability to repay these loans the peasant was forced to grow certain crops on terms decided by the creditor, selling at a price determined by the latter which was considerably below the market prices. On occasion the peasants needed the money long before the harvest time, forcing them to turn to the local Chinese monopoly money-lenders, in effect exchanging their future crops for buyers' credit at a very unfavorable price.

The peasant became a tenant on his own land; and especially by taking advantage of the peasants' needs during the money scarcity of the depression years in the 1930s the Chinese were able to exert an increasing control of the nation's crop land without having to own it. Unlike the United States, for example, where the financial interests were inclined to become big landowners which facilitated the introduction of modern technology for extensive land utilization, in Indonesia the financial interests did not themselves own the land, letting the peasant smallholders to continue with their labor intensive cultivation.

Originally the Chinese activities in trade, money-lending, and industrial activities were restricted by the Dutch to the coastal areas; in the beginning of this century, however, owing to growing pressures the restrictions were lifted and the remaining indigenous merchants and small village industry were subjected to unhampered Chinese competition. It was then followed by the disappearance of indigenous village industry; this destruction was further enhanced by the importation of mass-produced articles from Japan and the West.

Between the aristocratic elite and the mass peasantry among the indigenous population there was a middle class whose characteristics were unlike those of its counterpart in the presently developed economies. It has been remarked that "if one can speak of an Indonesian middle class, its entrepreneurial element had been almost eliminated by the circumstances attending three centuries of Dutch rule."[9] Thus "the last three decades of Dutch rule resulted in a rapid change in the over-all character of the tiny native middle class, its capitalistic element became smaller in proportion to a new and soon much larger group made up of government clerks, administrative officials (mostly of a junior grade) and teachers."[10]

Among the peasantry, its economic sense had been very dulled, a development which led some Dutch scholars to describe its twentieth-century mentality as still "pre-capitalistic."[11] The elite aristocracy, on the other hand, did not provide leadership nor did they mobilize resources for economic development; it had become instead the instrument for the exploitation of the native peasants. In economic decision making, the indigenous was on the whole at the periphery serving the central nonindigenous masters; in the enjoyment of the fruits of production activities, the indigenous mass was a spectator and an alien in its own native land.

Quality of Man

For economic purposes, the productive quality of man is determined by his education, learning, and opportunities to acquire experience and practice. Given the central-periphery relationship during the colonial period, the learning possibilities and the opportunities to acquire practice and experience were strictly limited. Newly independent countries found it difficult to rely completely on their own nationals to carry out the task of certain types of activities suddenly thrust upon them. In Tanzania, the attempt to replace expatriates with national personnel at an extensive rate might have been responsible for the delay in the plan implementation within the public sector.

In British West Africa, one of the few careers open to Africans had been law; though many could aspire to become a barrister, few would even dare to think of becoming a factory manager. Based on a government survey in 1928-29 of urban areas in Indonesia, it has been remarked that the figures "did not indicate that Western education was augmenting the economic development of native society"; furthermore, "of those Indonesians able to find employment where their education was used about 60 percent found it with the colonial government."[12]

While opportunities and possibilities for those who could successfully complete their education were limited, the aim and content of colonial education were not necessarily suitable for the requirements of a modern economy. The colonial systems of education had mainly been introduced to meet the type of manpower requirements for colonial economic structure and administration; it had been designed primarily to produce clerks for subordinate positions, possibly with little emphasis to making the natives well versed in Western culture and literature.

Emphasis was more on the literary rather than on technical expertise and vocational knowledge, which may have provided the colonial subjects with "the entry to the heritage of political and religious experience of mankind,"[13] but did not necessarily equip the country with skilled manpower. It had developed the attitude whereby "people tended to believe that the only genuine education was a literary one, and that any form of education which included some measure of practical training was inferior."[14] Furthermore, "manual labor was often felt to be undignified for the educated man."[15] In addition to the subordinate clerks, colonial education had produced articulate politicians, lawyers, literary critics, poets, who sometimes could not even communicate well enough in their own native language; on the other hand, it had produced little by way of people who could be directly productive, inventive, and innovative in its strictly material sense. Modern economy needs not only a critic who can extol the beauty of a piece of architecture; it needs architects who can model the building, surveyors to prepare the site, engineers, electricians, firemen, bricklayers, carpenters, plumbers, cement mixers, etc. Modern economy needs not only ministers of planning with adequately staffed bureaucratic and administrative structures which can guide, direct, control, and allocate projects; it also needs people who can be organized to carry out the projects.

As a very broad generalization, it might be suggested that there is a gap in the manpower quality of the developing countries: on the one hand, there are men who are extremely capable of assuming top leadership; on the other, there are men, constituting the majority, who are able to handle simple, purely menial jobs. The people in-between are not only scarce but probably more inclined toward the administrative framework. The problem might be translated into one of making the people able to perform jobs which require higher skills than the purely menial. Obviously it cannot be solved overnight for it is complex. However, one has to be careful not to mistake or confuse the identification of the problem. On the one hand, the scarcity of certain skills may be regarded as the cause of underdevelopment, in which case it constitutes bottlenecks and its elimination assures development. On the other hand, it may merely constitute symptoms of underdevelopment whereby the cause and its remedy have to be sought elsewhere. To confuse the latter with the former is a fallacy of misplaced concreteness.

It may be noted that if permissive factors and environment exist for developing new skills, the lack and absence of formal education need not constitute an insurmountable barrier. In the Soviet Union, many of the initial labor force recruited for the plants completed in the late 1920s were drawn from peasant and urban youths who could neither read nor write and possessed no skills and experience.[16] In the People's Republic of China, some factory managers were illiterate.[17] In the West, many industrial magnates had never attended a university.

On the other hand, although formal education, from primary school to university, has grown very rapidly in many developing countries in the wake of their independence, it has been observed especially with respect to Asian countries that "educational expansion has created excess capacity in certain categories of 'human capital' . . . in the midst of growing graduate unemployment there seems to be a genuine shortage of skilled people required for economic development."[18] Many of the educated unemployed have advanced specialized training, for example, in engineering.

Thus, in the face of its scarcity, there is a phenomenon of skilled manpower from the developing countries seeking and obtaining employment in the developed countries, a

phenomenon known as the "brain drain." A recent study
reports that the British reliance on medical manpower
from developing countries continues. The United Kingdom
relies on imported health personnel for one-quarter to
one-third of its medical staff needs. One-quarter of the
doctors working in the National Health Service were born
outside the United Kingdom. Forty-four percent of the
junior medical staff in the British National Health Service
comes mainly from India and Pakistan.[19]

Some students had been educated abroad on scholar-
ships paid for by governments or organizations on the basis
that they would return home. Some, like medical doctors,
had been totally or partly educated at home at highly
subsidized costs utilizing taxpayers' money. Some pre-
ferred to stay abroad for purely financial reasons. But
there are also others who have done so out of necessity
rather than choice. With the skills they acquired they have
not been able to find employment opportunities at home.
It is not unusual in some developing countries to find them
importing expatriate experts while their own nationals,
possessing equivalent expertise, are working elsewhere.

The problem regarding the productive quality of man
is, therefore, very complex. On the one hand is the
problem of assuring sufficient availability of skilled manpower to fill the posts required for carrying out production activities. On the other is the problem of creating
enough employment opportunities to prevent the existence of frustrated educated unemployed, which is not only
a waste to society, but it contains a potential social
explosive as well.

Nationalism and Economic Development

If the level of development is to be measured by the
level of *per capita* GDP, then the pace of economic
development is to be measured by its rate of growth.
However, as discussed earlier, this requires the acceptance
of a proposition that all that matters is its level, regardless

of how it has been generated and who is in control of its distribution. Colonialism has left the countries with economic dependence in their market orientation, and economic domination in their production process; a growth in their GDP, therefore, does not necessarily indicate an increase in the well-being of their nationals.

The nationalism of the 1940s and 1950s which energized the recently independent countries to struggle for political independence now is reasserting itself with an even greater drive to obtain economic independence, the greater degree of ability to determine the course of domestic economic events on their own terms and for their own interests. This requires nationally owned or controlled factors of production where the production sectors are nationally integrated, relatively flexible, and capable of self-generated and self-sustained growth. Clearly the modern economies are interdependent and no country could achieve full economic independence. But it is equally clear that Japan's dependence on the world market for imports of raw materials and exports of manufactures could not be regarded as in the same vein as Sudan's dependence on cotton exports and manufactured imports.

In these instances where the struggle for political independence was full of bitterness, this bitterness is in many cases still present in their society, and these countries have tended to avoid associating themselves with the former metropolitan countries in their economic development plans. This group includes Guinea and Algeria. On the other hand, those which evolved without deep bitterness to independence have remained in close contact and cooperation with their former metropolitan country. This group includes for the most part the former French colonies that are now closely united with France in OCAM.

It may be noted that greater amounts of aid and assistance could lead to a lesser degree of political independence. The break-off of relations with the United Kingdom over the Rhodesian issue, the insistence on the right to recognize an East German consulate, etc., all these had affected financial and technical assistance needed for the implementation of Tanzania's Five-year Plan. This is not to say that governments are wrong in imposing ties upon giving their financial and technical assistance; the primary responsibility of these governments is to look after their national interests, and it should not be expected that these coincide with the interests of the nationals of the recipient countries.

The same also applies regarding foreign investment and foreign capital.

In the midst of efforts made by the developing countries to attract them, there are charges that foreign corporations constitute parasitic enterprises extorting exorbitant economic exploitation. Here also the primary responsibility of these corporations is to the shareholders: there are premiums to be paid for taking risks and uncertainty and for investing capital, wherever they might be. The attempt to utilize moral standards while the reality has to be seen as it is, could lead to mutual mistrust, misunderstanding, and frustration.

In the early 1950s the nations of the West launched their development and aid programs for an increasing number of developing countries, partly because of the success of the Marshall Plan in Western Europe. Although there are few exceptions (not wholly attributable to the aid programs), they have not in general been very successful. A central factor for the lack of success was that the programs were conceived by the developed nations employing the *raison d'être* and the methodology of the industrialized countries. In the 1950s and the 1960s all the fundamental ideas, concepts, and methodologies have in general originated from the industrialized nations to be transplanted to the developing countries. The donors were quick to point out that some particular projects could not be financed because they were not in conformity with their preconceived notions and prescriptions.

On the other hand, much aid was wasted on particular

regimes in the developing countries which could not, and would not, carry out fundamental changes in their economies. Regardless of how well intended the programs had been, they sometimes represented paternalism, which is no longer tenable nor desirable.

If one were to review the plans of many of the developing countries, invariably one would notice the striking feature of their heavy reliance on foreign financing. Some were drawn by foreign experts, emphasizing techniques and a logically consistent framework for statement of intents rather than their relevance to economic and institutional realities of the developing countries. Many were merely a window-dressing framework for justifying requests for foreign aid. If they were based on a totally lacking concept of self-reliance, the inevitable might be difficult to avoid: the emergence of neocolonialism among the nominally independent countries.

The handicapped societies within the industrialized nations have had similar experiences. The American black ghetto, for example, was not turned into a productive community by outside aid. The new ghetto leadership boldly declares that outside aid not only did not transform their society, but as charity it lacked dignity. The new doctrine emerging from the black ghettos says: "Our goal must be to control our own lives—our own communities. We must have the dignity of being men." When a baby is born and starts growing, it needs a great deal of adult assistance, patience, support, and understanding. However, if it is continuously treated as an inferior and thus psychologically conditioned for the futility of self-reliance, it will remain an infant in its growth toward adulthood: the baby will grow but not develop into full manhood. One clear lesson of the aid programs of the 1950s and 1960s and in the welfare program of industrial societies for their ghettos, is that regardless of origin, without self-reliance they cannot do what is necessary for the transformation into a self-generating production entity. The concept that a foreign nation can transform a developing country purely through its assistance must be regarded as inaccurate.

The developed countries could provide the permissive factors, easing bottlenecks whenever they appear, but the basic framework and strategy for development have to be geared to the self-reliance of the developing countries themselves. The developing countries should be aware that regardless of the terms of foreign aid and foreign investment, there is the reality of its cost, at least in the forms of manifold ties, interests and amortization payments, and profits to be extracted.

As has been noted earlier, economic theory could lead to misleading conclusions: because income is low, savings are low and the only salvation is foreign capital inflow. Ethiopia and Tanzania, for example, are both predominantly agricultural and the *per capita* GDP in the latter is only about one-tenth higher: in 1966-68, the savings rate in Tanzania was more than twice the rate in Ethiopia; compared to 1960-62 figures, the savings rate in Tanzania has doubled while the rate in Ethiopia has slightly declined. With *per capita* GDP of $70, less than half the developing countries average, Tanzania has managed to save 21 percent of the GDP in 1966-68, greater than the developing countries average of 16 percent; unlike other developing countries with similar *per capita* incomes, Tanzania has to cope with a foreign-capital outflow instead of inflow, amounting to about 6 percent of GDP.

Per capita GDP in Japan during the Meiji era, converted at the postwar rate of exchange, was about $65. In the late nineteenth century about half the investment in the economy was undertaken by the government which extended protection to the landlords. Since the Meiji restoration, economic development was accompanied by considerable increases in agricultural output and productivity. Unlike some other developing countries Japan lacks natural resources: foreign currency acquired for industrialization was mainly raised through exports of raw silk to the United States, cotton fabrics and thread to other countries. In the form of its old system of feudal rice levies, Japan had considerable economic surplus converted into government revenue by the Meiji reforms. By the 1920's the investment rate in Japan was about 20 percent of the GDP. It could be noted that initially Japan was also subjected to a commercial treaty as was found in the colonized countries so that protective tariffs for industrialization could not be imposed. Rather than be resigned, the vigorous leadership carried out major reforms and revolutionized the institutional infrastructure: introduced a new tax structure, banking system, and legal framework; compulsory education; land reform; agricultural research, nationwide use of better seeds and fertilizer; started government enterprises and subsidized private industry. Japan did not rely on foreign capital, but instead it had a large, well-educated class of *samurai*, who were politically willing and able to introduce basic institutional changes, providing managerial and business leadership, bureaucratic expertise, and technical capacity.

The People's Republic of China before 1950 was a backward agricultural country continuously plagued by famine. China's level of *per capita* GDP, investment, and availability of infrastructure were possibly not as favorable as India's. China is now able to feed its people and is on the way toward being industrialized.

The experiences of Japan, China, the Soviet Union, etc., do not lead to the suggestion that the models could, and should, be duplicated elsewhere. Rather, they are illustrative of countries where strong and able leadership, based on self-reliance, have been able to carry out the transformation of their countries.

Leadership

The essence of any society is man: his well-being, outlook for the future, aspirations, and expectations. The goal of economic development is the increase in the state of the well-being of man; if the latter also includes mental, in addition to material, well-being, then the goal also includes human dignity and freedom from poverty, hunger, and illiteracy. If modernity is to be interpreted in the sense of the introduction and application of new or improved techniques of production as well as the efficient allocation of resources, then economic development necessitates modernity, but, given the existing traditional value system, the two need not be compatible.

Development which necessitates modernity requires changing old patterns and developing new ways of tackling economic and social problems; new conceptualizations which are not rooted to the traditional value system can be questioned for their relevance and might be strongly resisted or become ineffectual. The challenge of leadership in a democracy is to be able to play the role as an agent of economic development without jettisoning social unrest or upheaval.

Throughout most of the developing countries, there is a growing realization among the leaders that a socialized society would not only be efficient economically, but that it would also build upon the traditional collectivity and common family life of the people. At the same time, national leaders have rejected the blind acceptance of one type of socialized system in favor of pragmatic socialism. They are, on the contrary, seeking to adapt new methods and form new ideas that would be compatible with their own local traditions.

There are differences in the types of socialism practiced in the various developing countries, but practically all are seeking to preserve a value system which centers on primary consideration for the human person and emphasizes the obligation of society to assume responsibility of his well-being. Normative expectations of the leadership are often crystallized in explicit ideological formulations although in practice leaders often have to act on grounds of expediency and necessity, given the reality of the power structure.

The nature of the articulation, dissemination, and

implementation of ideology depends on the kind and effectiveness of political organizations which exist. Some countries opt for a one-party system while others for a multiparty structure. Regardless of the option chosen, leaders who are oriented toward economic development must find conceptualizations and formulas which can be formulated into an ideology for development. In the Soviet Union, Germany, and France, for example, the thrust of development was accompanied by a specific set of ideas about the cause and cure of economic backwardness.

During the colonial period, the leaders for independence were confronted with an identifiable focus and the problems could be reduced into how to mobilize the populace to drive out the colonial power, where programs and methods were clear-cut and implementable. Political rhetoric could successfully lead to political independence. Economic development, on the other hand, is much more complex. The problem is not resolved by merely declaring what is to be done; it requires well-formulated programs of how to do it, and a concept of who shares the cost and enjoys the benefits by how much. The leaders need the capacity for effective implementation of programs for the mobilization of resources to achieve economic development. Rhetoric of economic development would remain a rhetoric of economic development. Leadership does not only need to offer direction, it also needs the capacity to direct. Ideology for development is not sufficient to carry out the transformation into economic development.

In addition to the economic reality, economic development is inseparable from the reality of the power structure. Radical transformation makes extraordinary claims and demands sustained sacrifice on the part of the populace. It requires performance in the political arena as well as increasing national integration and national consciousness. It demands the acceptance of an idea that national interest is supreme.

Where indigenous private ownership of the means of

production is very little, power, wealth, and status are derived from political offices or government jobs. Since the party in power is the government in power, in this absence of alternative opportunity, government becomes the source of patronage for dispensing favor and income. The political party in this instance does not merely serve the political interest but the economic interest as well. In the face of the threat of a changing political fortune, the political party could clamor for the accumulation of funds for its treasury chest; thus, corruption might be institutionalized, but not necessarily because of private greed.

Corruption could spread to the lower ranking bodies of the government bureaucratic hierarchy through making the bureaucratic red tape unnecessarily complicated. Modern communications, although yielding considerable benefits, unfortunately enhance the appetite for conspicuous consumption at standards which generally could not be afforded in the developing countries by salary earnings alone. When corruption and graft are widespread as to become a *de facto* institution of public vice, when it becomes a normal rule rather than an exception, the government, instead of assuming the role as an agent of development, becomes a power structure which frustrates development efforts and initiatives.

On the other hand, aside from the ideological overtone, it is precisely because of the absence of indigenous private capitalists that it becomes imperative for the government to assume the role as an agent for economic development. The primary requirement is for the top leadership to have a high moral standard with a deep sense of commitment, dedication, and the responsibility which can be proud of its simplicity rather than in the display of wealth. The enforcement of accountability of public officials who misappropriate public funds would become a scene of comic opera if it is common knowledge that the people in the leadership are themselves corrupt.

While high moral standards and a deep sense of

responsibility, dedication, and commitment are all necessary conditions, they are not in themselves sufficient. The leadership must be able to set the goal and generate a passion for development without creating undue expectations; communicable, understandable, and acceptable to all strata of society as to convince them of the worthwhile nature of the concomitant sustained sacrifice required for their attainment.

This requires an apparatus for reaching all strata of society for disseminating goals and organizing efforts; a machinery for transforming general goals into local and national policies and then implementing them; an organization with communication channels (with the capability) to penetrate from the national center into the districts and below. Overcentralization might result in a long delay and the center being overburdened; decentralization, while it facilitates the system to be more responsive to local needs, could result in deflection from the basic goal at the local level.

Sustained sacrifice for the attainment of the goal of development cannot be maintained in the face of repeated failures. Implementation of projects and policies into tangible results requires specialized skills and expert knowledge. The quality of man in the developing countries is characterized by the gap between high- and low-level manpower. The middle-level manpower is lacking and cannot be expected to emerge as the natural outgrowth of the interaction of economic factors in the developing countries. It has to be consciously created to emerge.

This is the class of technocrats, people who acquire the managerial know-how, expert knowledge, and specialized knowledge, who are also in high demand in the developed countries. These people should be accountable only for their competence and abuse of power and not subjected to the tide of political fortunes. The developing countries are capable of producing this class as is witnessed in the phenomenon of the "brain drain." The problem is to motivate them into devoting their lives to work in their own countries.

NOTES

1. See H. Myint, "An Interpretation of Economic Backwardness," *Oxford Economic Papers*, June, 1954.
2. In the African context, see, for example, *Enlargement of the Exchange Economy in Tropical Africa* (United Nations publication, Sales No. 1954.II.C.4); *Scope and Structure of Money Economies in Tropical Africa* (United Nations publication, Sales No. 1955.II.C.4); *Structure and Growth of Selected African Economies* (United Nations publication, Sales No. 1958.II.C.4).
3. See O. Aboyade, *Foundations of an African Economy* (New York: Praeger, 1966).
4. See M. Yudelman, "Some Aspects of African Agricultural Development," in E. A. G. Robinson (ed.), *Economic Development for Africa South of the Sahara* (New York: St Martin's Press, 1964).
5. See D. North, *The Economic Growth of the United States: 1790-1860* (Englewood Cliffs: Prentice-Hall, 1961), p. 189.
6. See H. Myint, *The Economies of the Developing Countries* (London: Hutchinson, 1964).
7. See B. Higgins, "Elements in a Theory of Underdevelopment," in E. Nelson (ed.), *Economic Growth* (Austin: University of Texas Press, 1960), footnote 4, p. 66, for an illustration of the Indonesian case.
8. See G. M. Kahin, *Nationalism and Revolution in Indonesia* (Ithaca: Cornell, 1970), chap. I.
9. *Ibid.*, p. 29.
10. *Loc. cit.*
11. *Ibid.*, p. 2.
12. *Ibid.*, p. 30.
13. G. Hunter, *The New Societies of Tropical Africa* (London: Oxford University Press, 1962), p. 144.
14. K. Post, *The New States of West Africa*, rev. ed. (Baltimore: Penguin Books, 1968), p. 144.
15. *Loc. cit.*
16. See D. Granick, *Soviet Metal Fabricating and Economic Development: Practice versus Policy* (Madison: University of Wisconsin Press, 1967).
17. See E. L. Wheelwright and B. McFarlane, *The Chinese Road to Socialism* (New York: Monthly Review Press, 1970).

18. H. Myint, "Trade, Education and Economic Development," in I. G. Stewart (ed.), *Economic Development and Cultural Change* (Edinburgh: Edinburgh University Press, 1969), p. 8.
19. G. Henderson, *Emigration of Highly-skilled Manpower from the Developing Countries* (New York: UNITAR, Report No. 3, 1970), p. 28.

APPENDIX

TABLE I-1. SELECTED DEVELOPING COUNTRIES: LITERACY RATE, SECTORAL SHARES, SHARE OF MANUFACTURES IN TOTAL EXPORTS AND POPULATION[a]

Developing countries	Per capita GDP in dollars, 1967	Literacy rate[b]	Ratio to GDP (in per cent)[c]			Share of manufactures in total exports[d]	Population in millions, 1969
			Manufacturing industries	Industrial activity	Agriculture		
I. Countries with low literacy rate (20 per cent or less) and low manufacturing share (10 per cent or less)							
Rwanda*	46	10	4	5	69	0.1	3.5
Upper Volta*	49	7	6	6	55	4.0	5.4
Burundi*	52	10	4	4	72	...	3.5
Somalia*	61	5	4	...	...[e]	1.7	2.7
Ethiopia*	63	5	9	9	58	.6	24.8
Malawi*	66	15	8	9	38	1.2	4.4
Laos*	70	15	4	...	...[e]	...	2.9
Chad*	70	7	5	5	48	0.5	3.5
Tanzania, United Rep. of*	73	17	6	10	51	17.6	12.9

Dahomey*	83	10	7	7	53	12.0	2.6
Guinea*	87	5	6	20	35	..	3.9
Niger*	95	3	6	6	59	2.2	3.9
Mali*	88	2	8	8	48	1.1	4.9
Botswana*	99	20	8	8	47	..	.6
Sudan*	109	12	7	7	53	.1	15.3
Yemen*	110	10	3	..	..[e]	..	5.0
Central African Rep.	122	15	9	13	37	.6	1.5
Gambia	122	10	6	6	59	.0	.4
Sierra Leone	161	7	6	24	34	65.4	2.5
Mauritania	162	3	2	29	42	.9	1.1
Cameroon	163	12	8	20	51	3.1	5.7
Algeria	255	15	8	19	17	2.9	13.3
Iraq	273	20	9	41	21	1.7	9.3
Ivory Coast	279	20	9	12	41	5.4	4.2
Liberia	297	9	4	34	25	0.0	1.1
Zambia	316	17	10	45	9	.1	4.2
Gabon	504	12	4	25	22	7.8	.5

Appendix

TABLE I-1. (continued)

Developing countries	Per capita GDP in dollars, 1967	Literacy rate[b]	Ratio to GDP (in percent)[c]			Share of manufactures in total exports[d]	Population in millions, 1969
			Manufacturing industries	Industrial activity	Agriculture		
II. Countries with low literacy rate (20 per cent or less), high manufacturing share							
Nepal*	83	9	11	11	66	...	10.8
Haiti*	90	11	12	15	49	...	4.8
Congo (Dem. Rep. of)	83	15	17	25	19	19.0	17.1
Afghanistan*	88	8	11	11	45	8.1	16.5
Pakistan	129	19	11	12	47	50.5	111.8
Togo	133	7	11	21	47	3.8	1.8
United Arab Republic	187	20	...	24	30	25.5	32.5
Morocco	190	14	14	23	30	7.5	15.0
Senegal	217	6	14	14	33	4.8	3.8
Congo (People's Rep. of)	265	...	...	17	...	41.6	.9

III. Countries with low manufacturing share (10 per cent or less), high literacy rate

Nigeria	70	25	6	12	56	1.3	64.6
Burma	70	70	9	10	34	1.1	27.0
Lesotho*	85	40	1	3	68	. . .	.9
Indonesia	94	43	7	10	54	4.5	116.0
Uganda*	98	25	8	12	58	.7	9.5
Madagascar	116	35	5	13	53	5.9	6.6
Khmer Republic	134	58	10	17	41	.2	6.7
Jordan	267	32	8	11	22	15.1	2.2
Barbados	423	91	. . .	9	26	4.7	.2
Libya Arab Republic	1276	22	2	56	4	.0	1.9

* Listed as least developed countries.

a Three dots (. . .) indicate that data are not available.

b In the beginning of the 1960s. The figures refer to the proportion of the population fifteen years or over. For further notes, see World Economic Survey, 1969-1970, p. 205.

c 1967 or earliest available estimates.

d 1968 or earliest estimates. Figures refer to the SITC items in Sections 5 to 8, with the exception of iron and steel (67) and non-ferrous metals (68).

e Data not available but assumed by the Committee for Development Planning to be under 10 per cent.

Source: World Economic Survey, 1969-1970; Yearbook of National Accounts Statistics, 1969, Vol. II; Handbook of International Trade and Development Statistics, Supplement 1970; Monthly Bulletin of Statistics, June, 1971, and estimates based on data from national and international sources.

TABLE I-2. TOTAL AND AGRICULTURAL ECONOMICALLY ACTIVE POPULATION AND GROSS VALUE ADDED PER ECONOMICALLY ACTIVE POPULATION IN THE RESPECTIVE SECTORS IN SELECTED DEVELOPING COUNTRIES, 1967

Country	Economically active population as percent of total population, earliest estimate	Percentage of agricultural economically active population, earliest estimate	Gross value added per economically active population in U.S. dollars[a]		Ratio of gross value added per economically active population in percent	
			Total	In agriculture	Agriculture to total	Agriculture to other sector
I. Low-manufacturing; low-literacy						
Rwanda	40	95	116	85	73	12
Upper Volta	53	87	92	58	63	18
Burundi	50	95	103	78	76	14
Somalia	36	89	169	..	..	..
Ethiopia	37	88	168	111	66	19
Malawi	31	81	210	99	47	14
Laos	..	81	..	..	..	..
Chad	45	92	156	81	52	8
Tanzania	37	95	199	107	54	6

Dahomey	53	84	156	98	63	21
Guinea	49	85	176	72	41	10
Niger	29	97	323	197	61	4
Mali	:	90	:	:	:	10
Botswana	46	91	214	111	52	9
Sudan	47	86	233	144	62	19
Yemen	:	:	:	:	:	:
Central African Republic	37	:	325	:	:	:
Gambia	:	:	:	:	45	:
Sierra Leone	43	75	374	168	:	17
Mauritania	:	:	:	:	:	:
Cameroon	:	:	:	:	34	:
Algeria	22	50	1175	399	44	20
Iraq	28	48	965	425	47	29
Ivory Coast	50	86	559	263	31	11
Liberia	40	81	733	227	11	8
Zambia	30	81	1036	114	26	2
Gabon	50	84	998	259		5

TABLE I-2. (continued)

Country	Economically active population as percent of total population, earliest estimate	Percentage of agricultural economically active population, earliest estimate	Gross value added per economically active population in U.S. dollars[a]		Ratio of gross value added per economically active population in percent	
			Total	In agriculture	Agriculture to total	Agriculture to other sector
II. High-manufacturing; low-literacy						
Nepal	46	94	181	127	70	12
Haiti	56	83	160	94	59	20
Congo (Dem. Rep.)	50	86	167	37	22	4
Afghanistan	25	87	353	183	52	12
Pakistan	35	68	370	255	69	42
Togo	44	..	303	..	..	..
United Arab Republic	30	57	621	329	53	32
Morocco	28	56	679	360	53	34
Senegal	42	..	512	..	..	..
Congo (People's Republic)	..	..	..	..	..	..

III. Low-manufacturing; high-literacy

Nigeria	33	..	213	..	..	..
Burma	..	..	..	..	..	..
Lesotho	51	..	165	..	..	..
Indonesia	36	68	262	207	79	55
Uganda	37	89	265	172	65	17
Madagascar	50	84	230	152	66	21
Khmer Republic	44	80	307	157	51	9
Jordan	23	35	1166	723	62	52
Barbados	38	24	1113	1191	107	111
Libyan Arab Republic	26	37	4984	548	11	7

[a]Computed from GDP at market prices, 1967.

Source: FAO, Production Yearbook; ILO, Yearbook of Labour Statistics and Table I.